Bringing Out the Best in Teachers

SECOND EDITION

What Effective Principals Do

Joseph Blase
Peggy C. Kirby

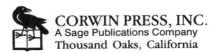
CORWIN PRESS, INC.
A Sage Publications Company
Thousand Oaks, California

For information:

Corwin Press, Inc.
A Sage Publications Company
2455 Teller Road
Thousand Oaks, California 91320
E-mail: order@corwinpress.com

Sage Publications Ltd.
6 Bonhill Street
London EC2A 4PU
United Kingdom

Sage Publications India Pvt. Ltd.
M-32 Market
Greater Kailash I
New Delhi 110 048 India

Printed in the United States of America

Library of Congress Cataloging-in-Publication Data

Blase, Joseph
    Bringing out the best in teachers: What effective principals do / by Joseph Blase, Peggy C. Kirby.—2nd ed.
        p. cm.
    Includes bibliographical references and index.
    ISBN 0-8039-6861-2 (cloth: acid-free paper)
    ISBN 0-8039-6862-0 (pbk.: acid-free paper)
    1. Teacher-principal relationships. I. Kirby, Peggy C. II. Title.
LB2840 .B57   2000
371.1'06—dc21   99-6348

03 04 05 06 7 6 5 4 3

Corwin Editorial Assistant: Kristen L. Gibson
Production Editor: Denise Santoyo
Editorial Assistant: Nevair Kabakian
Typesetter/Designer: Lynn Miyata
Cover Designer: Ravi Balasuriya

Bringing Out the Best in Teachers

SECOND EDITION

*To the teachers who participated in
the study on which this book is based,
to the outstanding principals they described,
and to Dale and Evan for their patience.*

Contents

Foreword to the First Edition   vii
by Arthur Blumberg

Foreword to the Second Edition   x
by Roland S. Barth

Preface to the Second Edition   xii
  Acknowledgments   xiv

About the Authors   xv

1. Principals and Their Effectiveness   1

2. The Power of Praise   11

3. Influencing by Expecting   23

4. Influencing by Involving   41

5. Granting Professional Autonomy   59

6. Leading by Standing Behind   69

7. Gentle Nudges: *Suggesting Versus Directing*   83

8. Positive Use of Formal Authority   95

9. Mirrors to the Possible   105

10. Conclusions, Caveats, and Challenges   119

    Resource A: Research Methods and Procedures   131

    Index   137

Foreword to the First Edition

*M*ost research and writing concerning school principals and their influence on teachers and schools has been on the principals themselves. "Listen to what *they* say," we seem to have been thinking, "and we'll find out how things ought to happen in school."

That position contains a certain amount of truth, but it leaves out a vital type of information—that which involves the way *teachers* see the behavior of their principal, particularly the behavior that seems to motivate them to try to do a better job, to become involved in the problems of the school, to reflect on their work, and so forth. This book is an important step in filling that void. Metaphorically, it has been waiting in the wings for some time.

Implicitly, in researching and writing this book, Joseph Blase and Peggy Kirby have moved closer to dealing with the question, "What is 'the proper study' of school administration?" Much as the proper study of humankind is the human animal and its institutions, the proper study of school administration is school administrative practice. In order to study something, the rule is, get as close to it as you can. Blase and Kirby have tried to use that rule in their research; what has resulted is a welcome addition to the literature of administrative practice.

As I read the book, the thought that occurred to me over and over was that I was being invited by the authors and by the teachers involved in the study to reflect on some essential elements of administrative practice. If I were a principal, how and when would I praise my teachers, for example? What is the character of the expectations I hold for my teachers and how would I communicate those expectations? Would I, for instance, simply tell them at the beginning of the school year and at a few subsequent faculty meetings that I expect them to hold high standards for themselves and their students and let it go at that? Or, am I aware that my behavior all day long carries a much more powerful message than the words I speak on formal occasions? Am I aware, as the authors state in a very powerful notion, that I, as a principal, place myself on public exhibition all day, every school day?

Practicing and would-be school principals will have a lot to mull over if they permit themselves to use this book, not as simply a cookbook of administrative recipes, but as a means of thinking about what they do and how and why they do it. In this regard a caveat, which Blase and Kirby take note of several times, is necessary. It is that the strategies or techniques employed by a principal take on their most essential meaning through the motives, the hopes, the intentions—the leitmotif—of the user. Put another way, it is the basic rhythm that the principal communicates through his or her use of strategies that is really important. The words are of little value without the music—this seems to be the prepotent message.

Another kind of message emanates from this book, although I don't think that Blase and Kirby had it in mind when they wrote it. It is a message that is directed at academics, particularly those whose careers focus on doing and reporting research in educational administration. Sadly, as most practitioners will tell you, the research in educational administration has had minimal effect on practice. The doing of research in administration has, for the most part, been a plaything of professors. It is taken seriously only with regard to matters of promotion and tenure. And, for sure, concerns with matters of practice are to be avoided. They are too prosaic to be given much research-oriented thought. Perhaps I exaggerate, but only for effect.

In the chapters that follow, Blase and Kirby highlight one way to do respectable academic research that focuses on practice. So I would suggest that professors who come across this book give it very thoughtful heed.

This book is full of little "sleeper" thoughts. Here is one that ought to occupy the thinking of both principals and professors for some time. It comes in the form of a teacher's reflection on a new principal:

> She has a very positive feeling about our school. She enjoys her job and it is reflected to the rest of the teachers. . . . She faces every day as a new day with new challenges. I try to do the same. I don't mind coming to school this year. When the alarm goes off, I'm "up and at them." (p. 102)

The book has numerous ideas like this that poke themselves into the careful reader's consciousness. Principals will certainly benefit from reading and thinking about them. The thoughtful research-oriented professor could probably build a career or two studying them. As a starter, what are the words and music that one finds in a school where the teachers are "up and at them"? Be careful, though, because in another school the words and music may be different—but have the same effect.

—Arthur Blumberg
Professor of Educational
Administration and Supervision
Syracuse University
Syracuse, New York

Foreword to the
Second Edition

*W*hen I was a principal, I came to understand that teachers are capable of both their best and their worst. I saw my job as trying to discover and then provide the conditions under which each of us was likely to bring our best into the schoolhouse. A daunting task at times.

Fortunately, this is precisely what this revised edition of *Bringing Out the Best in Teachers* is all about: Recognizing that the principal is the prime builder of either a healthy or a toxic school culture and then showing us how to unlock the best in teachers and avoid the worst.

How do you unlock the best in teachers most of the time? For an answer, the authors turn to teachers themselves. And that is the power of this little volume.

Leadership is ultimately in the eyes of the led. A principal may comply with all 64 of the characteristics of an effective leader as seen by the state department of education, but if the teachers don't experience their principal as a leader, then the principal isn't one. Conversely, what teachers do experience as leadership is good leadership. The importance of this book is that it allows us to see through teachers' eyes.

Most people would agree that one of the most important responsibilities of a school principal is to create a school ethos in which the personal and professional development of adults will flourish. But the principal as staff developer can become unilateral, even paternalistic. I am delighted that these authors have turned the idea of professional development within the schoolhouse on its head. What you are about to encounter are the voices of many, many teachers who have become the staff developers of aspiring and practicing principals. When I think of it, this reversal should come as no surprise. For without question, I learned most about the turbulent, difficult, heroic job of school leadership from the teachers with whom I worked each day.

I even know of a few courageous principals who periodically invite their teachers to appraise their leadership systematically—to evaluate them. The principals report helpful, yeasty, growth-producing feedback and insights that give new meaning to the phrase *transformational leadership*. The chapters that follow lend themselves beautifully not only to self-appraisal but to this kind of collective appraisal as well.

I join with Peggy Kirby and Joseph Blase in inviting you to anoint teachers as your staff developers. The clear and imaginative voices of teachers that you are about to experience have much to teach us about wise, effective, humane school leadership.

—Roland S. Barth
Winter 1999

Preface to the Second Edition

$\mathcal{T}$his book is for school principals—both practicing and prospective—who want to bring out the best in teachers. It is intended to help them examine, rather specifically, what they can do to influence teachers and their performance. Unfortunately, the relationship between school leadership and its effects on teachers and their work has not been explored fully in the educational literature. This literature tends to be quite abstract and often misses many of the important and concrete elements that make up the everyday world of the school. The practical and prescriptive literature is not adequately informed by solid empirical research. Moreover, the simplistic recipes for effectiveness that are typically offered offend practitioners who understand full well the complex nature of school leadership, teaching, and learning. On both counts, it is hoped that this book will be a relief.

Bringing Out the Best in Teachers is based on an in-depth study of the everyday strategies that open and effective school principals use to influence, motivate, and empower teachers. It is written entirely from the teacher's perspective, a perspective that has largely been ignored in the administration literature. The research approach used to collect the data for this book allowed teachers to identify and describe freely, in their own words and in great detail, how effective principals influence them and exactly how such influence affects their teaching and, more generally, their work with students. In this second edition we review additional recently published literature. In so doing, it is evident how timely the study that is the basis of this book remains.

Here you will find detailed portrayals of what effective principals actually do—from the teacher's point of view—that leads to improved teacher motivation, commitment, and innovation and enhances teachers' abilities to achieve high academic and social goals with students. The descriptions from the teachers' reports are presented in a straightforward and understandable way. We wrote this book on the premise that administrators have a better chance of developing meaningful ways of working with teachers if they take the opportunity to reflect critically on their leadership within the context of knowledge produced from a study of teachers' perspectives on effective leadership.

Many physical and psychological barriers make interaction and communication between administrators and teachers difficult. Teachers are physically and psychologically isolated from administrators; their desire for autonomy increases this isolation. Principals face overwhelming demands for their time, and their formal authority is limited. Teachers, therefore, may choose to disregard school principals whose goals and strategies of influence are inconsistent with school goals and teachers' professional norms and expectations. When teachers' and principals' purposes and strategies are incongruent, a climate is created that prevents them from reaping the benefits (such as elevated levels of teacher motivation and commitment) that effective leadership can have for them and, indirectly, for students.

What kinds of principal-teacher interaction do produce these benefits? The heart of this book—Chapters 2 through 9—describes the strategies and related practices employed by open and effective principals to enhance teachers and their work with students. Principals' goals in using the strategies and the specific consequences for teachers are fully described. Each chapter closes with a set of guidelines for the reader's consideration.

In Chapter 1, we present a brief overview of research on the principalship and a description of the research methods employed. Chapters 2 and 3, respectively, focus on the importance of praise and how principals articulate expectations to effect changes in teacher thinking and behavior. In Chapter 4, we examine the many ways principals involve teachers in instructional and noninstructional decisions. Chapter 5 describes how, by extending autonomy to teachers, principals are able to enhance teachers' development. Several strategies—including the use of rewards and principal support—are discussed in Chapter 6. Indirect, subtle, and yet powerful strategies—including giving advice, providing opportunities for professional development, and distributing professional literature—are explored in Chapter 7. Chapter 8 considers the consequences of employing formal authority to ensure teacher compliance. In Chapter 9, the significance of three personality characteristics (consideration, optimism, and honesty) and two strategies (modeling and visibility) are highlighted. Chapter 10, the final chapter, challenges the reader to consider the applicability of the leadership strategies discussed herein for school restructuring.

This book discusses some fine, even extraordinary, principals whose dynamic leadership has had remarkably positive effects on teachers and, we suspect, on students as well. It describes these principals as seen through the eyes of teachers. The book shows what happens when school principals work to create open, honest, and sincere relationships with teachers. Principals who have studied and used the strategies discussed in this book tell us that they were able to create school environments that focus on the social and educational welfare of students and that such schools are possible because they bring out the best in teachers.

Acknowledgments

Several principals and teachers provided valuable feedback on earlier drafts of this book. We are deeply grateful for their incisive and constructive comments and for the overwhelming enthusiasm they expressed for this project. We wish to thank Lewis Allen, Michael Bochenko, Sherry Dungan, Laura Lester, Terry Lock, Lewis McAfee, Judy Meloy, Fred Oliver, Kathy Singleton, Paul Smith, and Terry Poor for their assistance. Special thanks go to Jo Blase for her assistance with literature reviews and Chapter 1.

—Joseph Blase
University of Georgia

—Peggy C. Kirby
University of New Orleans

About the Authors

*J*oseph Blase is Professor of Educational Leadership at the University of Georgia. Since receiving his degree in 1980 from Syracuse University, his research has focused on understanding the work lives of teachers. He has published many studies in the areas of teacher stress, relationships between teachers' personal and professional lives, teacher socialization, and principal-teacher relationships. During the past several years he has published widely on school-level micropolitics. His work concentrating on school-level micropolitics received the 1988 Davis Memorial Award given by the University Council for Educational Administration.

He edited *The Politics of Life in Schools: Power, Conflict, and Cooperation* (winner of the 1994 Critic's Choice Award, sponsored by the American Educational Studies Association); coauthored, with Jo Blase, Gary Anderson, and Sherry Dungan, *Democratic Principals in Action: Eight Pioneers* (1995); coauthored, with Gary Anderson, *The Micropolitics of Educational Leadership* (1995); and coauthored with Jo Blase, *The Fire Is Back: Principals Sharing School Governance* (1997) and *Handbook of Instructional Leadership: How Really Good Principals Promote Teaching and Learning* (1998). His numerous articles appear in journals such as the *American Education Research Journal* and *Educational Administration Quarterly*.

*P*eggy C. Kirby is Professor of Educational Leadership and Foundations and University Research Professor at the University of New Orleans, where she teaches graduate courses in research and school leadership. She is a certified teacher and program evaluator in the

state of Louisiana. Since receiving a PhD in educational administration in 1987, she has investigated school-level factors, particularly leadership and governance, that influence student and teacher
outcomes. Through her work with the University of New Orleans
Principals' Center and the Georgia League of Professional Schools,
she has assisted school leaders in examining and implementing
alternative forms of governance based on teacher empowerment.
She is Chair of the Board of Directors of the Jefferson Coalition for
Alternative Schools and cofounded the Jefferson Community
School, Louisiana's first charter school that serves middle school
students at risk of failure due to chronic discipline problems. She
coauthored, with Vincent Anfara, Jr., *Voices from the Middle: Decrying
What Is, Imploring What Could Be* (1999). Her research publications
have focused on alternative middle schools, shared leadership, ethics in educational administration, and classroom processes related
to effective schooling, and have appeared in journals such as the
American Journal of Education, the *Journal of Educational Administration,* and the *Middle School Journal.*

Principals and Their Effectiveness

One's identity is defined less by a job description, as in the
old bureaucratic ideal, than by one's relation at any given
moment to groups and people.
                        —*Leinberger & Tucker (1991, p. 350)*

*B*oth scholars and practitioners of educational administration
believe that principals play a critical role in schools. Many argue
that school principals can affect virtually all aspects of school life.
Yet, empirical research provides few detailed pictures of the everyday social and behavioral dynamics of effective school-based leadership. This is especially true with regard to understanding leadership
from the perspective of teachers and, in particular, how school
leadership enhances teachers and their overall performance. This
book helps fill the gap by adding to the knowledge about how open
and effective principals influence teachers and to the specific consequences of this influence for teachers.

Fueled by the effective schools research and school reform of the
late 1970s and 1980s, the interest in understanding effective princi-

pals has increased significantly. Studies conducted during the last two decades have highlighted a host of factors associated with strong school leadership. These include initiative, confidence, tolerance for ambiguity, analytic abilities, resourcefulness, vision, democratic-participatory style, listening, problem centeredness, openness, time management skills, high expectations, knowledge of curriculum, and ability to allocate resources effectively (e.g., Blase, 1987; Blumberg & Greenfield, 1986; Bossert, Dwyer, Rowan, & Lee, 1982; Brady, 1985; Brookover & Lezotte, 1977; Edmonds, 1982; Hallinger & Murphy, 1987; Hannaway & Stevens, 1985; Lipham, 1981; Russell, Mazzarella, White, & Maurer, 1985).

There is little question that this group of studies has added to our knowledge about effective principals. At the same time, few published studies (e.g., Blase & Blase, 1994; Peterson, 1978; Wolcott, 1973) have focused more broadly on principals and what they do. Indeed, concrete descriptions of how effective school principals use a wide range of strategies to influence teachers and their work are not available (two exceptions, which focus more specifically on instructional aspects of effective leadership, are Blase and Blase, 1998, and Reitzug, 1997).

A study completed by Russell et al. (1985) at the University of Oregon describes effective principal behaviors and links them to the characteristics of effective schools. These authors note, for instance, that principals who provide extra academic work for outstanding students or who encourage students to take highly challenging courses contribute to the characteristics of high expectations and clear school goals. These researchers report more than 100 such effective principal behaviors.

Bossert et al. (1982) contributed greatly to our understanding of the relationship between leadership and teacher performance by introducing a model that links school principals' actions—such as goal setting, evaluating, monitoring, and modeling—to instructional climate (i.e., staff commitment, discipline) and instructional organization (e.g., academic curriculum and pedagogy). Student achievement outcomes are viewed as an indirect result of principals' actions that affect instructional climate and classroom organization. The theoretical model discussed by Bossert et al. has been more recently tested by Heck and his associates (Heck, Larsen, &

Marcoulides, 1990; Heck & Marcoulides, 1993). They found several behaviors, including communicating instructional goals, working to keep faculty morale high, and establishing an orderly environment, that enhance school climate. Other leadership behaviors—developing school goals, securing resources for programs, evaluating curricular programs—were identified with promoting instructional organization. Heck and his associates demonstrated that the two classes of leader behavior (i.e., instructional climate and instructional organization) positively affected student achievement in the schools they studied. Their conclusions regarding the importance of a range of informal principal behaviors is consistent with the teachers' data we discuss in this book. They write:

> Our results indicate that many of the important instructional leadership variables influencing school achievement are not related to the regular clinical supervision of teachers. . . . While regularly observing teachers and conferencing with them regarding instructional improvement is admittedly an important aspect, our results show that principals' time and attention are focused on a variety of additional activities. Many behaviors which are more informal and strategic cluster into the constructs of instructional organization and school climate and impact student achievement as well. Some of these efforts involve clarifying, coordinating, and communicating a unified school educational purpose to teachers, students, and the community. Effective principals appear to build a sense of teamwork at the school. (Heck et al., 1990, pp. 120-121)

In sum, although the study of instructional aspects of leadership and student achievement has been shown to be complex and empirically challenging (Hallinger & Heck, 1996a, 1996b), and although a number of scholars have acknowledged the dearth of studies of the relationships among leadership, teaching, and student achievement (Leithwood, Begley, & Cousins, 1990), some direct and indirect links to student achievement have been found.

Principals' Influence on Teachers

More specifically, studies conducted during the last three decades of how school principals use power and influence in their interactions with teachers have helped to advance understanding of school-based leadership. In this group of studies, principal effectiveness has been associated with the use of positive forms of influence with teachers rather than formal authority. Isherwood (1973) found that principals who demonstrate charisma, expertise, and human relations skills heighten teachers' loyalty to the principal and improve teacher satisfaction. Studies have shown how principals have granted teachers direct participation in decision making and consistently professed confidence in teachers' abilities; the latter often include initiation of teacher leadership in schools (Allen, Glickman, & Hensley, 1998; Crow, Matthews, & McCleary, 1996; Riordan & da Costa, 1998). Furthermore, building trust has been shown to be a key leadership behavior (Short & Greer, 1997), just as principals' use of persuasion is significantly related to the degree of consensus that teachers perceive in schools (Muth, 1973). Hanson (1976) discovered that in innovative schools, public praise by administrators results in desired modifications of teacher behavior. Hanson also found that principals who describe appropriate professional conduct positively influence teachers.

Studies of principal influence have shown how important informal power is to working effectively with teachers. Treslan and Ryan (1986) learned that teachers are much more responsive to principals' influence attempts based on human relations skills and technical expertise than to the use of hierarchical authority. Administrators' attempts to define school values (Firestone & Wilson, 1985), interpersonal competencies (Blase, 1987; Blumberg & Greenfield, 1986; Bredeson, 1986), support (Brady, 1985; Hoy & Brown, 1988; Reiss & Hoy, 1998), and vision (Blumberg & Greenfield, 1986), for instance, were found to be very effective in influencing teachers. Leithwood and Jantzi (1990) and Blase and Blase (1998) found that principals who rely on such strategies as staff development, communication about values, power sharing, and the use of symbols are able to foster collaborative relationships among teachers. Johnson (1984) and Blase and Roberts (1994) indicate that expertise, personal example, distribution of resources, and expressed interest favorably affect teachers. Johnston and Venable (1986) link participatory decision making to greater teacher loyalty to principals. High and Achilles (1986) conclude that such behaviors as enabling, norm setting, and expertise are effective means of influence with teachers in high-achieving schools. With regard to effects on teachers' commitment, involvement, and innovativeness, Sheppard (1996) learned that promoting teachers' professional development is the most influential leadership behavior at both the elementary and the high school levels. Finally, recent studies of the broad approach of transformational leadership have found a relationship between leadership behaviors and the existence of an effective, collaborative, innovative school culture (Conger & Kanungo, 1994; Leithwood, Tomlinson, & Genge, 1996; Sergiovanni, 1992).

Some Concluding Remarks

Some noteworthy gains have been made toward understanding the principal-teacher relationship, especially as it relates to influence. Most of the studies noted, however, focus on teachers' and/or principals' perceptions of the types of power that principals use. These studies correlate types of administrative power with a limited number of variables, such as teacher satisfaction or loyalty, rather than focusing on effective principals per se. One qualitative study examines the "general" perspectives of effective principals (Blumberg & Greenfield, 1986); it does not investigate how principals influence teachers. Another qualitative study focuses specifically on the communication styles of principals vis-à-vis teachers (Bredeson, 1986). More directly, three qualitative studies completed by Hanson (1976), Leithwood and Jantzi (1990), and Blase and Blase (1994) explore different aspects of principal influence in relation to teachers; each generates some data regarding strategies. In contrast to the study discussed in this book, none of these three studies produced detailed descriptions of the range of strategies that typical principals use to influence teachers' growth and development; nor did the first two produce data regarding the effect of strategies reported.

The data presented in the following chapters were taken from a larger qualitative study that investigated teachers' perceptions of the strategies used by all types of principals to influence them. This total database was subsequently divided into strategies employed by open and effective principals and those used by principals whom teachers viewed as closed and ineffective.

The data discussed throughout this book focus specifically on understanding teachers' perspectives regarding only the strategies used by open and effective principals. Consistent with open-ended research methods, no definitions of "open and effective" were presented on the questionnaire that teachers completed for the study. Doing this would have limited teachers' freedom to discuss their own views of open and effective principals. The study also explored teachers' views about why they considered the strategies used by principals to be effective, as well as the purposes (goals) they attributed to principals' use of such strategies.

In addition, our study examined the effect of school principals on the cognitive, affective, and behavioral aspects of teachers' work. To our knowledge, no research has used qualitative research methods to investigate the full range of strategies that principals typically employ in their work with teachers or the consequences of such strategies for teachers themselves. A large sample of teachers participated in the study, thus adding to the credibility of the findings. The open-ended questionnaire used to collect data was administered to over 1,200 teachers. Of these, 836 focused on the strategies used by open and effective principals. Analysis of the questionnaires produced detailed descriptions of 1,323 strategies used by effective principals. It is this portion of the total database from which this book was written. (See Resource A for a full description of the research problem, sample, and procedures.)

This book discusses the strategies used by effective principals and how such strategies positively influence teachers. Generally speaking, the strategies appear here in terms of the frequency with which they were reported, from most frequent to least frequent. Chapters 2 through 9 describe the effective strategies and related tactics and practices, and their effect on teachers. Guidelines for reflection drawn from the research data are presented in the closing pages of each chapter. Although each chapter focuses on only certain influence strategies, we must emphasize that effective and open principals used most of the strategies described throughout this book. In the final chapter (Chapter 10), we present conclusions from our research and challenge the reader to reflect on the applicability of the strategies of open and effective principals in restructuring the schools of tomorrow. The methods used to collect and analyze the data we used for this book are discussed in Resource A.

Note: We wish to acknowledge Jo Blase for her contributions to this revised edition and to the authorship of this chapter.

References

Allen, L., Glickman, C., & Hensley, F. (1998, April). *A search for accountability: The League of Professional Schools.* Paper presented at the annual meeting of the American Educational Research Association, San Diego.

Blase, J. (1987). Dimensions of effective school leadership: The teachers' perspective. *American Educational Research Journal, 24*(4), 598-610.

Blase, J., & Blase, J. (1994). *Empowering teachers: What successful principals do.* Thousand Oaks, CA: Corwin.

Blase, J., & Blase, J. (1998). *Handbook of instructional leadership.* Thousand Oaks, CA: Corwin.

Blase, J., & Roberts, J. (1994). The micropolitics of teacher work involvement: Effective principals' impacts on teachers. *Alberta Journal of Educational Research, 40*(1), 67-94.

Blumberg, A., & Greenfield, W. (1986). *The effective principal: Perspectives on school leadership* (2nd ed.). Boston: Allyn & Bacon.

Bossert, S., Dwyer, D., Rowan, B., & Lee, G. (1982). The instructional management role of the principal. *Educational Administration Quarterly, 18*(3), 34-64.

Brady, L. (1985). The supportiveness of the principal in school-based curriculum development. *Journal of Curriculum Studies, 17*(1), 95-97.

Bredeson, P. V. (1986, April). *Principally speaking: An analysis of the interpersonal communications of school principals.* Paper presented at the annual meeting of the American Educational Research Association, San Francisco.

Brookover, W., & Lezotte, L. (1977). *Schools can make a difference.* East Lansing: Michigan State University, College of Urban Development.

Conger, J. A., & Kanungo, R. N. (1994). Charismatic leadership in organizations: Perceived behavioural attributes and their measurement. *Journal of Organizational Behaviour, 15,* 439-452.

Crow, G. M., Matthews, L. J., & McCleary, L. E. (1996). *Leadership: A relevant and realistic role for principals.* Princeton, NJ: Eye on Education.

Edmonds, R. R. (1982). Programs of school improvement: An overview. *Educational Leadership, 40*(3), 4-11.

Firestone, W. A., & Wilson, B. L. (1985). Using bureaucratic and cultural linkages to improve instruction: The principal's contribution. *Educational Administration Quarterly, 21*(2), 7-30.

Hallinger, P., & Heck, R. H. (1996a). Reassessing the principal's role in school effectiveness: A review of empirical research, 1980-1995. *Educational Administration Quarterly, 32*(1), 5-44.

Hallinger, P., & Heck, R. H. (1996b). The principal's role in school effectiveness: An assessment of methodological progress, 1980-1995. In K. Leithwood, J. Chapman, D. Corson, P. Hallinger, & A. Hart (Eds.), *International handbook of educational leadership and administration* (pp.723-783). Dordrecht, The Netherlands: Kluwer.

Hallinger, P., & Murphy, J. (1987). Instructional leadership in the school context. In W. Greenfield (Ed.), *Instructional leadership: Concepts, issues, and controversies.* Boston: Allyn & Bacon.

Hannaway, L., & Stevens, K. (1985, April). *The indirect instructional leadership role of a principal.* Paper presented at the annual meeting of the American Educational Research Association, Chicago.

Hanson, M. (1976). Beyond the bureaucratic model: A study of power and autonomy in educational decision making. *Interchange, 7*(1), 27-38.

Heck, R. H., Larsen, T. J., & Marcoulides, G. A. (1990). Instructional leadership and school achievement: Validation of a causal model. *Educational Administration Quarterly, 26*(2), 94-125.

Heck, R. H., & Marcoulides, G. A. (1993). Principal leadership behaviors and school achievement. *NASSP Bulletin, 77*(553), 20-28.

High, R., & Achilles, C. M. (1986). An analysis of influence-gaining behaviors of principals in schools of varying levels of instructional effectiveness. *Educational Administration Quarterly, 22*(1), 111-119.

Hoy, W. K., & Brown, B. L. (1988). Leadership behavior of principals and the zone of acceptance of elementary teachers. *Journal of Educational Administration, 26*(1), 22-38.

Isherwood, G. B. (1973). The principal and his authority: An empirical study. *High School Journal, 56*(6), 291-303.

Johnson, N. A. (1984). *The role of the Australian school principal in staff development.* Unpublished master's thesis, University of New England, Armidale, New South Wales.

Johnston, G. S., & Venable, B. P. (1986). A study of teacher loyalty to the principal: Rule administration and hierarchical influence of the principal. *Educational Administration Quarterly, 22*(4), 4-27.

Leinberger, P., & Tucker, B. (1991). *The new individualists.* New York: Harper Collins.

Leithwood, K., Begley, P., & Cousins, B. (1990). The nature, causes, and consequences of principals' practices: An agenda for future research. *Journal of Educational Administration, 28*(4), 5-31.

Leithwood, K., & Jantzi, D. (1990, April). *Transformational leadership. How principals can help reform school cultures.* Paper presented at the annual meeting of the American Educational Research Association, Boston, MA.

Leithwood, K., Tomlinson, & Genge, M. (1996). Transformational school leadership. In K. Leithwood, J. Chapman, D. Corson, P. Hallinger, & A. Hart (Eds.), *International handbook of educational leadership and administration* (pp. 785-840). Dordrecht, The Netherlands: Kluwer.

Lipham, J. (1981). *Effective principal, effective school.* Reston, VA: American Association of School Principals.

Muth, R. (1973). *Teacher perceptions of power, conflict, and consensus. Administrator's notebook.* Chicago: Midwest Administration Center.

Peterson, K. (1978). The principal's tasks. *Administrators' Notebook, 28*(8), 1- 4.

Reiss, F., & Hoy, W. K. (1998). Faculty loyalty: An important but neglected concept in the study of schools. *Journal of School Leadership, 8,* 4-25.

Reitzug, U. C. (1997). Images of principal instructional leadership: From supervision to collaborative inquiry. *Journal of Curriculum and Supervision, 12*(4), 356-366.

Riordan, G., & da Costa, J. L. (1998, April). *Leadership for effective teacher collaboration: Suggestions for principals and teacher leaders.* Paper presented at the annual meeting of the American Educational Research Association, San Diego, CA.

Russell, J. S., Mazzarella, J. A., White, T., & Maurer, S. (1985). *Linking the behaviors and activities of secondary school principals to school effectiveness: A focus on effective and ineffective behaviors.* Eugene: University of Oregon, Center for Educational Policy and Management.

Sergiovanni, T. J. (1992). *Moral leadership: Getting to the heart of school improvement.* San Francisco: Jossey-Bass.

Sheppard, B. (1996). Exploring the transformational nature of instructional leadership. *Alberta Journal of Educational Research,* 42(4), 325-344.

Short, P. M., & Greer, J. T. (1997). *Leadership in empowered schools: Themes from innovative efforts.* Upper Saddle River, NJ: Merrill.

Treslan, D. L., & Ryan, J. J. (1986). Perceptions of principals' influence bases. *Canadian Administrator,* 26(2), 1-7.

Wolcott, H. (1973). *The man in the principal's office: An ethnography.* New York: Holt, Rinehart & Winston.

The Power of Praise

When I am in [the principal's] office taking care of business and he sees me, or when I peek into his office to say hello, he takes time to give me some kind of feedback. Sometimes it is as casual as "You look peppy today." Sometimes it is to comment on something I'm involved in: "The Drill Team sure was impressive last night. How cohesive, proud, and disciplined they looked!" He'll tell me about a student's comment that I have a lot of energy and organizational skills which make my class fun.

The main thing, no matter what he says, is he is sincere. It's not B.S. and isn't dished out just for the sake of it . . . Credibility is important. I'm not sure he does this consciously . . . it's just the way he is. He has good interpersonal skills, and that probably carries him a long way and is responsible for his effectiveness.

I feel good, inspired, motivated. It reminds me that it sure is easy to make someone's day, and we need to take time to [do so] more often. Being motivated makes us do a better job. I'm sure it helps me remain positive and flexible.

—*A high school teacher*

*O*f all the strategies used to influence teachers' work, praise was the most frequently reported and was perceived as one of the most effective by teachers in our study. Interestingly, only in recent years has praise appeared in descriptions of effective school leadership (Blase & Blase, 1994; Blase & Blase, 1997; Murphy & Louis, 1994).

Our teachers, however, clearly recognized the value of personal compliments and individual attention from their principals. Why then the discrepancy between what teachers perceive to be such a crucial role for principals and what school effectiveness researchers discuss as key correlates of leader effectiveness?

Perhaps, as Greenfield (1987) hints, it may be taken for granted that principals routinely praise teachers. After all, teacher performance assessment instruments invariably include indicators of how teachers reinforce student behavior; positive reinforcement is universally accepted as a correlate of effective teaching. Principals, as former teachers, may be expected automatically to translate this teaching behavior to the leadership domain. That some principals are effective in doing so is revealed in our data. Nevertheless, praise remains conspicuously absent in the literature about effective instructional leadership. For this reason, it may be underused by school principals.

Perhaps principals are familiar with the power of praise, but in their haste to attend to the research-recognized components of instructional leadership, the importance of praising teachers may be displaced. Terrence Deal (1987) was among the first to recognize that the school effectiveness literature (with regard to the principal's role) ignores important aspects of schools. He argues that schools should be examined through multiple lenses. Principals must attend to other critical organizational dimensions in addition to instruction. They must be instructional leaders as well as counselors or parents, engineers or supervisors, contenders or referees, and heroes or poets. As counselors/parents, principals add to personal growth and development with praise, advice, and affection. The nurturing function, according to Deal and other scholars (e.g., Beck & Murphy, 1994; Deal & Peterson, 1990; Evers, 1992) is one of the most time-consuming demands of the principalship. Unfortunately, principals who are eager to develop their "instructional leadership" skills may do so at the expense of advancing their interpersonal relations with teachers.

Viewing principals as counselors or parents, as Deal (1987) suggests, may appear a bit paternalistic to many teachers, thereby reducing teachers' stature. Even if Deal's analogy is scorned, his counsel nonetheless may be valid. We reiterate that in our data, praise is the most frequently mentioned influence strategy used by open and effective principals. Its role in leader effectiveness should not be ignored or taken for granted.

Why Praise?

Given that principals are expected to assume many roles in schools and that the role of instructional leader alone is a multifaceted one, why do effective principals devote so much time to praising teachers? Although one intent in conducting this study was to identify effective strategies used by principals to influence teacher performance, it may be true that praise also satisfies personal needs of the principals themselves. From several studies of successful school principals, Blase and Blase (1994, 1997, 1998) learned that such principals have high needs for expressing and receiving affection and warmth. Principals who are successful may be sensitive to the interpersonal needs of teachers because they themselves derive satisfaction similarly.

In addition to the personal satisfaction they may derive from praising teachers, according to our data, effective principals also use praise as a strategy for influencing teachers' attitudes and behavior. Teachers in our study linked the use of praise specifically to principals' goals of promoting and reinforcing classroom performance. As an influence strategy, praise is used most often with individual teachers; open and effective principals commend teachers for their instructional and classroom management efforts. Recognition of individual teachers' strengths is viewed as a means of maintaining and developing teachers' skills while promoting teachers' confidence and satisfaction.

Whereas other influence strategies are intended to encourage teachers' involvement in aspects of schooling that transcend the classroom, goals associated with the use of praise are related primarily to enhancing instructional performance. Praise also is used (but less frequently) to build school climate, faculty cohesiveness, and support for school goals.

Teacher Reactions
to the Use of Praise

We have all heard the occasional grumblings of administrators uncomfortable with overt displays of affection or encouragement; they claim not to be the "touchy-feely" type. Similarly, we have heard the teacher who disdains such expressions of approval, viewing them as condescending or patronizing. Is the use of praise necessary and effective for improving teaching performance? To answer this question, we again turn to the responses of our teachers.

The teachers in our study viewed praise as a positive and effective influence strategy. Praise from their principals helps boost their confidence and pride. Many reported that positive reinforcement left them feeling "encouraged," "appreciated," and "recognized":

> The principal often writes personal notes to individual faculty members, encouraging, complimenting, and just giving "strokes." These are found in our mailboxes at school or sometimes sent out to our homes. She also sends out notes to the entire faculty complimenting them for a job well done. She makes me feel that what I do is appreciated, and these actions give me positive thoughts about the principal . . . I know how busy her schedule is. When I feel that what I do is noticed and appreciated, I have a better feeling about my job and try to do a better job.
>
> —*A middle school teacher*

In addition to promoting greater esteem and satisfaction, the use of praise increases teachers' sense of belonging. Because their principals take the time to recognize their contributions, teachers feel that they are "important members of the team." Others said they feel "loved" and "respected" by their principals.

As a strategy for influencing teacher behavior, the use of praise is particularly successful. Teachers reported that the positive feelings associated with praise lead to increased motivation. They feel "inspired" and "enthusiastic." Their loyalty and dedication grows. Because of her principal's appreciation, one teacher declared, "I wouldn't think of not doing a good job. I would feel guilty." Another concurred: "I try to do my best to live up to his comments."

Praise affects teacher behavior along several dimensions. Generally, teachers attempt to comply with the expectations of principals implied in the use of praise. According to teachers, performance compliance concerns instruction and use of time:

♦ "I try harder to be creative in my teaching."

♦ "Indeed, more time is spent planning."

♦ "I work harder. This means I don't just put in 8 hours a day. I work until I'm finished."

Recognizing how praise positively affects them, teachers often model the practice by using a more positive discipline approach, including frequent praise, with students. Modeling is used both in the classroom and throughout the school building:

♦ "I'm more positive . . . open and patient with students."

♦ "I look for something to praise the kids about."

♦ "I find myself trying to emulate [the principal's] positiveness not only with my students but with parents and other teachers."

Finally, teachers reported that praise affected their support for principals. Some teachers acknowledged reciprocating:

♦ "I praise him in return."

♦ "I'm quicker to support the principal."

Others volunteered their time and energy to help principals:

♦ "I'll do 'extras' for her."

♦ "I'm more apt to volunteer for projects she needs help on."

It appears then that praise is an effective strategy for improving school climate because it enhances teacher morale and teachers' attitudes toward students. It also enhances teachers' instructional practices and the amount of effort they put forth.

On Potency and Ubiquity

Our research has produced indisputable evidence of the power of praise as an influence strategy with teachers. We have suggested that some educators—teachers and principals—may feel uncomfortable with this strategy. Still, we cannot deny its potency. We have gathered substantial evidence of the positive effects of praise on both attitudes and behaviors of teachers. Two questions surface with regard to this finding. First, how do we account for the singular effect of a strategy that may be viewed as "obvious" or "common sense"? And if the potency of the strategy is obvious, why is it not used by more school principals?

Educators invariably agree that their work is plagued by difficulties. Means and ends are only loosely connected; seldom are we certain that what we actually do in the classroom positively affects students' lives. In one of the most respected studies of the sociology of teaching, Dan Lortie (1975) observed that teaching is filled with "endemic uncertainties" related to difficulties of assessing individual student outcomes and the quality of teaching, as well as of multiple role expectations (pp. 134-161). Because the link between what teachers do and its effect on students is uncertain, teachers must rely on self-evaluations of performance. Yet most individuals have needs for recognition and approval that remain unfulfilled by self-evaluation alone. Other studies confirm the existence of similar problems for teachers (Blase & Blase, 1998; Lieberman & Miller, 1984; Rosenholtz & Simpson, 1990).

Uncertainties and self-doubts could be mollified by approval from others. Unfortunately, formal performance evaluations, no matter how outstanding, offer teachers little consolation. A positive evaluation indicates minimal competence; seldom is it used for purposes of recognition or advancement. And, as Lortie (1975) notes, veteran teachers work day after day knowing that they can be replaced by novices!

Because teaching also is characterized by the isolation of the classroom, there are few opportunities for interaction with other adults. Teachers rarely observe or are observed by other teachers. They spend nearly every working minute communicating with children—often as many as 150 children per day. It is not surprising that they respond so appreciatively and enthusiastically to adult interaction and feedback. Unless cooperative experiences such as peer coaching become commonplace, administrators are the only external adult referents by which teachers judge their work.

Perhaps the most revealing observation from our study is that teachers reported being influenced by praise only when it was related to their professional performance. Although they may have been complimented for appearances (e.g., a new suit or hairstyle) or praised for accomplishments outside the school, only work-related praise was reported as a source of influence. To be effective with teachers, it seems, praise must be connected to professional accomplishments.

Earlier, we asked the question, "Why praise teachers?" The more obvious question now seems to be, "Why not?" Unfortunately, the same barriers that inhibit teacher interaction also limit teacher-administrator communication. With many teachers to observe, each in a different enclosed location, even informal assessments of teacher performance are time-consuming. But to reinforce positive teacher behaviors, observation is mandatory. (What would we praise them for if we did not find out how well they were doing?) Thus, even for principals who value informal classroom visits and are comfortable expressing compliments and gratitude, the demands on their time are exacerbated by the structural isolation of teaching. Nevertheless, despite the difficulties in observing and acknowledging classroom performance, some principals are particularly adept at recognizing teacher contributions to school success.

Opportunities and Methods

How and when do effective and open principals praise teachers' professional performance? The answer, according to our teachers: Principals capitalize on every available opportunity to compliment teachers; their praise consists of brief but sincere remarks and gestures.

Although time and structure may limit the number of opportunities to praise individual teachers, open and effective principals take advantage of other situations. Many teachers reported that their principals regularly use group praise. Principals are able to reach many teachers at once by complimenting them at faculty meetings, in conferences with smaller groups of teachers, or over the intercom. As evidenced by the remarks of several teachers, principals use such occasions to express praise without qualification:

- ◆ "He expresses a complete faith and belief in his faculty . . . says we are the chosen ones . . . the best faculty in the state."
- ◆ "He starts and ends every meeting by complimenting the faculty for their hard work."
- ◆ "Every Friday she tells us how hard we worked."

We learned from our study that praise can be an effective influence strategy even when it is not communicated directly to teachers. Teachers reported knowing how their principals feel about their work from comments the principals made to others. Although perhaps not intended as a means of influence, teachers did learn of these remarks to others and were impressed by them. As one teacher boasted, "He brags on us every chance he gets."

<u>Group praise is not, we found, used by effective principals to compensate for a lack of individual praise.</u> Quite the contrary, principals intersperse frequent and specific individual praise with group praise. They mention individuals by name at faculty meetings and in conversations with others. Informal verbal compliments are commonplace; one teacher called them "1-minute praises." Another noted the deliberate effort of his principal to praise teachers: "She catches me doing something right and says so." Although principals most often comment on some aspect of teacher performance that they have witnessed, compliments from students or parents also are relayed to teachers.

In addition to oral praise, the principals described in our study wrote brief notes to individual teachers. After observing classes, many principals left brief notes of praise on teachers' desks. Others placed complimentary notes in the mailboxes of individual teachers.

Finally, principals often express praise nonverbally. Especially effective during the classroom observation where the principal hopes to be unobtrusive, the nonverbal gesture communicates immediate approval. This technique takes several forms, all appreciated by our teachers:

♦ "She touches me on the shoulder to show her appreciation."
♦ "A few literal pats on the head are one of his strategies."
♦ "Simple smiles tell me a lot."

Thus, effective principals rely on brief, usually informal, verbal and nonverbal praise to influence individual teachers and teacher groups. It should be noted that variety and frequency of praise appear to be as important as the particular techniques used (e.g., written memos, comments to others, public address announcements, pats on the back). It is important to stress that teachers in our study often spoke of praise not as an influence strategy used by a principal, but as a part of the principal's character. Praise is sincere, genuine, and even natural for these principals. Rinehart, Short, Short, and Eckley (1998) found that teachers' perceptions of their own empowerment is positively influenced by principals' social influence. Concern for teachers' work and support of that work are key principal characteristics related to teachers' belief in their own empowerment.

Tips From Teachers

Our data indicate that in spite of the endemic uncertainties and structural isolation of teaching, effective principals find many opportunities to commend teachers and that, to be effective, praise need not be formal or lengthy. The particular behaviors for which the teachers in our study were praised also are revealing. In every case reported, teachers indicated that the praise that influenced them most was evoked by their work. Thus, on the basis of our teachers' reports, we offer the following suggestions to consider in the context of your own school setting.

1. Praise sincerely.

Teachers view praise from effective principals as genuine. Rather than perceiving it only as an influence strategy, teachers see its expression as comfortable and natural for their principals.

Praise does not appear contrived or awkward; it is congruent with other behaviors and personal characteristics of principals.

2. Maximize the use of nonverbal communication.

Effective principals use nonverbal gestures such as smiles, nods, and touches to communicate approval. Although not used as an exclusive form of praise, this technique is commonly employed during classroom observations to avoid the disruption of verbal praise.

3. Schedule time for teacher recognition.

Many teachers report that their principals praise them on a regular basis. Some principals choose the beginning or the end of faculty meetings. Recognition of faculty at student assemblies also is common. Others choose to announce faculty accomplishments over the public address system at the end of each week. Many principals routinely praise teachers during their tours of schools. It is clear that open and effective principals build time for praise into their busy schedules. Although the use of praise seems "natural," the neophyte might become more adept at the use of this strategy by consciously scheduling opportunities for recognition. As the practice becomes automatic and comfortable, additional forums for praise might be added.

4. Write brief personal notes to compliment individuals.

To praise individual teachers, effective principals often rely on written messages. These brief notes are always handwritten and personalized. The teachers in our study did not report being influenced by written acknowledgment of group efforts.

5. Show pride in teachers by boasting!

Teachers often learn of their principals' judgments of their work from others. Principals express pride in their teachers to parents, colleagues, and others in the community.

6. Praise briefly.

To be effective, praise need not be formal or lengthy. Teachers appreciate many forms of recognition that last only seconds. Thus, short accolades delivered in a variety of forums using both verbal and nonverbal techniques can be effective without placing excessive demands on the principal's time.

7. Target praise to teachers' work.

Because of the isolation and uncertainty characteristic of the profession, teachers are most responsive to praise bestowed for school-related success. Whenever possible, principals should commend specific professional accomplishments of individual teachers. Group praise can be used to increase the opportunities for recognition, but it too should be tied to specific achievements.

References

Beck, L. G., & Murphy, J. (1994). *Ethics in educational leadership programs: An expanding role.* Thousand Oaks, CA: Corwin.

Blase, J., & Blase, J. (1994). *Empowering teachers: What successful principals do.* Thousand Oaks, CA: Corwin.

Blase, J., & Blase, J. (1997). *The fire is back: Principals sharing school governance.* Thousand Oaks, CA: Corwin.

Blase, J., & Blase, J. (1998). *Handbook of instructional leadership: How really good principals promote teaching and learning.* Thousand Oaks, CA: Corwin.

Deal, T. (1987). Effective school principals: Counselors, engineers, pawn brokers, poets . . . or instructional leaders? In W. Greenfield (Ed.), *Instructional leadership: Concepts, issues, and controversies* (pp. 230-245). Boston: Allyn & Bacon.

Deal, T., & Peterson, K. (1990). *The principal's role in shaping school culture.* Washington, DC: Department of Education.

Evers, C. W. (1992). Ethics and ethical leadership: A pragmatic and wholistic approach. In P. A. Duignan & R. J. S. MacPherson (Eds.), *Educative leadership* (pp. 21-43). London: Falmer.

Greenfield, W. (1987). Moral imagination and interpersonal competence: Antecedents to instructional leadership. In W. Greenfield (Ed.), *Instructional leadership: Concepts, issues, and controversies* (pp. 56-73). Boston: Allyn & Bacon.

Lieberman, A., & Miller, L. (1984). *Teachers, their world and their work: Implications for school improvement.* Alexandria, VA: Association for Supervision and Curriculum Development.

Lortie, D. C. (1975). *Schoolteacher: A sociological study.* Chicago: University of Chicago Press.

Murphy, J., & Louis, K. S. (1994). *Reshaping the principalship: Insights from transformational reform efforts.* Thousand Oaks, CA: Corwin.

Rinehart, J. S., Short, P. M., Short, R. J., & Eckley, M. (1998). Teacher empowerment and principal leadership: Understanding the influence process. *Educational Administration Quarterly, 34,* 630-649.

Rosenholtz, S., & Simpson, C. (1990). Workplace conditions and the rise and fall of teachers' commitment. *Sociology of Education, 63,* 241-257.

Influencing by Expecting

The main tactic used by my principal in trying to influence us is emphasizing that what we do is "for our babies." For example, the county did not have a breakfast program, and our principal thought we should. This is a very economically depressed area, and she saw a need to enhance the nutritional well-being of our children. There was resistance to this from the educational community, but her general emphasis on "our babies" being taken care of in every way was the power of her argument which proved successful.

[As a result,] I find all my thoughts are on the children and what I can do to totally enhance their school experience. We all concentrate our efforts on the children. Because [the principal] is sincere in her commitment to children, I feel proud and privileged to be associated with her and her ideas.

—An elementary school teacher

*H*igh expectations for student academic achievement is prominent on any list of effective schools characteristics (e.g., Edmonds, 1979; Purkey & Smith, 1983). The expectations of students, parents, teachers, and administrators are all positively related to student outcomes (Brookover, Beady, Flood, Schweitzer, & Wisenbaker, 1979; Glenn & McLean, 1981; Rutter, Maugham, Mortimore, Ouston, & Smith, 1979; Teddlie, Falkowski, Stringfield,

Desselle, & Garvue, 1984; Weil et al., 1984). Not surprisingly, there is often a consistency about expectations among these multiple groups: When parents, teachers, and principals hold high expectations for students, students are likely to expect more of themselves (Heck, Larsen, & Marcoulides, 1990; Heck & Marcoulides, 1993; Sheppard, 1996).

More specifically, the influence of principals' expectations on student achievement has been investigated by school effectiveness researchers. The expectations that principals hold for both student performance and teacher performance are positively related to student academic success (Austin, 1979); even so, causal statements regarding the role of principal expectations in influencing student achievement cannot be made. Logic tells us that this role is probably an indirect one: Few principals have time to interact directly with students on a daily basis. Teachers provide the obvious link. Communication with teachers about expectations for students has been heralded as a critical component of school climate that affects student outcomes (Heck et al., 1990).

At first glance, we may conclude that principals' expectations have a power somewhat like the ominous warnings in chain letters. Teachers feel convinced or compelled to pass the principal's "message" along to their students. The principal's expectations mushroom as teachers spread the word to their awaiting charges.

We know that expectations regarding ability, aptitude, values, and pedagogy are not accepted unquestioningly, however. Teachers do not passively adopt their principal's values and beliefs and translate these into compatible teaching behaviors that, in turn, affect student performance. The chain letter metaphor breaks down because any understanding of the principal's influence must take into account individual teacher differences in values and understandings. Principals' expectations for changes in teacher attitudes and behavior gain meaning and derive influence only as they are interpreted and evaluated by teachers.

Expectations for What?

Our data indicate that effective principals use expectations to achieve two broad goals: changes in attitudes and changes in behaviors. Principals are aware of their own limitations in influencing teacher attitudes; they assume that changes in attitudes often follow changes in teacher behavior. A teacher reported that her principal, for example, believes very strongly in the benefits of reserving time blocks for reading. How can the principal use expectations to influence teachers to use this new method? As we see it, she has two options: She can expect teachers to see the importance of the method (a change in attitude), or she can expect teachers to try the method (a change in behavior).

Our findings suggest that effective principals attack from both fronts. They recognize that some teachers are influenced by expectations because they perceive the principal as having expert knowledge in an area or because they are drawn in by the principal's personality. For other teachers, however, seeing is believing; changes in their attitudes result from their own evaluation of a new method as it is implemented. We learned that open and effective principals communicate the expectation that their teachers "give things a chance" before passing judgment.

Consider two statements to teachers regarding a silent reading program:

♦ "I expect student test scores in reading to increase if students are given uninterrupted reading time each morning."

♦ "I expect you and your students to read silently for 15 minutes each morning."

The first statement, it seems, is intended to convince teachers of the value of silent reading; behavioral changes are only implied. The second is intended to change teachers' behavior (time allocation) regardless of their attitudes. It appears that effective principals recognize the separate and collective effect of both kinds of statements; thus, they frequently use expectancy statements aimed at changing both attitudes and behaviors.

What are the specific goals of principals who want to change the attitudes and behavior of teachers? Although expectations occasionally reflect school district policies and programs, our data indicate that the expectations of open and effective principals are largely derived from their personal values regarding appropriate human interaction and school purposes. These principals are not mere messengers of expectations for district directives; they communicate their own personal visions of ideal school climate and processes related to respect for students, teacher classroom behavior, teacher-parent communication, curriculum, and pedagogy. As we discuss in later chapters, however, effective principals involve teachers in setting school goals. Thus, the expectations they convey are shared by others in the school community. Consequently, the entire school community (not just the principal) is responsible for leadership through expectation (Ackerman, Donaldson, & van der Bogert, 1996).

Respect for Students

Respect for students is a prominent theme evident in the language and behavior of effective principals. Teachers are expected to demonstrate respect and encourage student self-esteem. Principals associate these behaviors with both improved student discipline and achievement.

Teachers report that they are expected to use directed praise; that is, students' individual strengths are to be highlighted to project respect. Nonspecific praise (e.g., "Erin, you're doing so much better") should be replaced with clarification of both expectations and perceived outcomes ("Ramon, I'm so pleased that you're remembering to cross out the identities to simplify your fractions").

Recognizing and accepting individual differences is another important aspect of respect for students. Teachers stated that effective principals encourage them to "find something good" in each student. Very often, recognition programs are developed in academic and nonacademic realms. For instance, one principal videotapes classrooms to enhance student self-esteem—all the students present thus are able to admire themselves at work. Other principals recognize students for good citizenship. Many create possibilities for a variety of students to achieve such rewards. Asking two typically "detached" students to remove trash from the play area during recess and later publicly recognizing their accomplishment is one such tactic.

Respect for underprivileged students is often an explicit goal of open and effective principals described by our teachers. Teachers are expected to treat all students with dignity. Effective principals work to enhance teachers' sense of efficacy in dealing with students of all backgrounds. No student is presumed incapable of learning or improving. Teaching efficacy goes beyond a belief in one's own competence in terms of knowledge and skills (Dembo & Gibson, 1985; Tschannen-Moran, Hoy, & Hoy, 1998). In a study of school climate and efficacy, Lasserre (1989) found that in schools where there were greater incentives for professionalism and an emphasis on hard work and dedication, teachers reported higher levels of teaching efficacy. Echoing the findings of earlier efficacy studies (e.g., Armor et al., 1976), Lasserre concludes that a successful education program reflects a belief that all students can learn and that principals' expectations can influence that belief.

Teacher efficacy contributes to greater effort and persistence, according to Tschannen-Moran, Hoy, and Hoy (1998). Increases in teacher efficacy have been associated with principals' willingness to provide resources and buffer teachers from disruptive factors (Lee, Dedick, & Smith, 1991), model appropriate behavior and provide rewards for performance (Hipp & Bredeson, 1995), improve school climate (Hoy & Woolfolk, 1993), and initiate and support meaningful staff development (Blase & Blase, 1998).

Influencing Teacher Behavior

Another purpose associated with the use of expectations is the modification of teacher behavior. In some cases, efforts to modify teacher behavior are related to expectations that teachers convey respect for students. For example, teachers describe effective principals as expecting them to "control their tempers." They are expected to model the kind of behavior expected of students and to demonstrate a "dignified," "positive approach" to student discipline.

Effective principals also use expectations to influence other aspects of school climate, including faculty relations. They often speak of the cohesiveness of their faculties, the idea of "family," and of "being in this together." Kouzes and Posner (1990) refer to this as a way of "enlisting others." These authors further note the effect of language in "giving life" to an expectation. Less effective principals say "I believe all students can learn." Unconvinced principals even deny that the belief is theirs: "Research says that . . ." The language of the effective principal, however, denotes conviction as well as an expectation: "We know that all students can learn." Of course, effective principles will deny neither their own values nor empirical evidence, but they do use language ("we") to encourage unity.

Teacher-Parent Communication

The use of expectations to influence teacher behavior is not limited to school climate factors. Principals also use expectations to enhance school-home communication. The goal is conveyed both overtly and suggestively. Teachers report that effective principals frequently encourage contact with parents. One principal placed telephones in the faculty lounge to emphasize his expectations about communicating with parents.

Curriculum and Pedagogy

Expectations are effectively used to communicate goals for programs, curriculum, and teaching methods. Earlier we mentioned a principal who emphasized the value of reading by implementing a silent reading program. Changes in scheduling were used to reinforce the verbal message that all teachers were expected to support this program.

Preference for particular teaching methods often is revealed in the expectations of the effective principals that teachers described. Through their words and actions, teachers know whether their principals favor, for instance, direct instruction, exploratory learning, or peer coaching. One teacher described the principal as having a definition of education that he explicitly differentiated from training to influence teachers to use more creative instructional methods:

> He believes that schools must teach students how to make a living and how to live productive, meaningful lives. He constantly stresses the importance of using our classrooms to do more than train students. They must provide students with opportunities to learn to discriminate between valid and invalid information. He has made me aware that every

student needs both [training and education], and only if we make this distinction will we have a balance in our educational system.

With a renewed emphasis on mastery of basic skills, there are more and more classrooms where urban poor children engage in what can best be described as "choral yelling." Under the enthusiastic direction of their overzealous teachers, they recite (or lip-sync!) multiplication facts, language rules, or dates in history. Memorization is equated with mastery. Not so in the school of our "education" principal. It is highly unlikely that a single teacher in this school will be found "directing the chorus."

Teacher Effects

How do teachers feel when their principals expect them to think and act in particular ways? And, more important, do the expectations of principals result in any real changes in the way teachers subsequently think and act?

Our teachers told us that the subtle (and not-so-subtle) messages communicated by open and effective principals are generally clear, consistent, direct, and tactful. As such, teachers tend to view the strategy very positively; they are pleased because they hear the strength of conviction and see an ability and willingness on the principal's part to model appropriate behavior. Blase and Blase (1998) found that successful principals treat teachers with respect, act on their own values and beliefs rather than in compliance with bureaucratic roles, and hold themselves accountable for their school's success. Because successful principals are willing to practice what they preach, they engender higher levels of faculty satisfaction, motivation, and efficacy. Teachers in our study also reported great responsiveness to principals who communicate and model clear and consistent expectations.

Teacher behavior and attitudes indeed are affected by principal expectations. Our findings disclose that principals' expectations enhance teachers' sensitivity to and respect for students in matters of discipline. Teachers report practicing greater self-control, consistency, and fairness in such matters. They also take on extra duties in response to their principals' expectations. One teacher started a weekly newsletter because of the principal's emphasis on school–home relations. Another spent personal time helping with a food drive (initiated by the principal) for victims of a hurricane.

Teachers reported that they usually conform to principals' expectations; they had both rational and pragmatic reasons for doing so. In the first case, they appreciate knowing what's expected, what's important, and what's valued. In the second case, they associate the use of expectations with positive outcomes such as being able to "see students and faculty growing."

Some of the teachers included in our study seem to rationalize that the benefits of complying with their principal's expectations outweigh the disadvantages. They recognize the positive outcomes of using expectations to influence other teachers, and sometimes explain that "it's not because of me" that the approach is necessary. Similar to many teachers' attitudes toward evaluation, their belief is that other teachers need more guidance and monitoring. In explaining how she felt about the principal's use of expectations to influence her behavior, one teacher stated, "I feel stressed and overwhelmed, yet I am glad that those teachers who were not performing are now forced to put up or shut up."

The negative feelings we found with regard to the use of expectations are not surprising. New expectations tax the psychological and physical strengths of teachers. When attitudes change, they must be assimilated into the existing values structure; when behaviors change, they usually displace previous behaviors. Using that phone in the lounge to call six parents during a teacher's only free time during the day may mean that he cannot score those 147 tests his students took today, which may mean that he has to skip that PTO meeting, which his principal expects him to attend . . .

A few of our teachers were cynical about complying with principals' expectations. They saw themselves as "playing the game" and going along with what the principal wanted without becoming personally involved or committed. Nevertheless, our research suggests that the rumblings of the occasional cynic are invalidated by the teachers who report new insights or a more reflective stance because their principals dare to challenge the status quo.

Yes, But . . .

Through our work with teachers we have been convinced that principals do have direct influence on teacher attitudes and behaviors. Teachers attest to this influence, and when working with effective and open principals, teachers are generally pleased with the changes in school climate and organizational processes that ensue. Teachers themselves have reported improvements in their interactions with students, their use of time, their teaching methods, their communication with parents, and their sense of belonging.

Our research provides strong evidence linking principals' use of expectations to improved teacher behavior. Equally important is the ability of this conclusion to inform practice. We are sure that the reader is now likely to be thinking "Yes, but . . ." "But how can I use this to change our (we hope you didn't say *my*) school?" "But who will be convinced just because I say I 'expect' something?" "But exactly how do these open and effective principals do it?" Those in fact are the questions that must be answered if we hope to improve practice. We must identify the specific tactics (e.g., behaviors, practices) used by effective principals to convey and achieve what they expect to convey and achieve.

The Language of Expectations

The most obvious strategy for communicating expectations is the use of words. Our data indicate that effective principals choose a variety of words to indicate their desires. In addition to, and often preferable to, "I expect . . ." are "Let me clarify . . .," "I want to emphasize . . .," "I encourage you to . . .," and "I'd like to explain . . ."

Our teachers reported that expectations are reinforced through repetition, clarification, and consistency. It is not enough to assert at an afternoon faculty meeting that problem-solving skills are to be incorporated into every subject area. Bombarded with new information on a variety of topics after a long day in the classroom, teachers are selective in what they choose to attend to and what they choose to ignore. When a new idea or philosophy is presented, some teachers (and principals) tell us that they usually assume that "this too shall pass." The "problem-solving approach" is filed away in that part of the brain that stores fuzzy musings on nongraded classes and democratic learning. Only when the notion is mentioned again and then again is it retrieved for further processing. In a world characterized by information overload, repetition is the key to influencing action. It is not that teachers are defiant; they simply have been conditioned to attend selectively to new information.

Whereas repetition reveals the degree of importance that principals attach to their messages, clarification seems to improve the likelihood that teachers will be able to act. The principal who expects teachers to implement a problem-solving approach clarifies what he or she means by problem solving and what he or she expects in terms of implementation. Is this to be the only approach used? Does it require a new curriculum or new materials? Are all teachers expected to use the method? Repetition then is enhanced by rephrasing and informing.

Finally, language is evaluated for its consistency. The principal who sends mixed messages with regard to his or her expectations dilutes the probability of successfully influencing listeners. In a study sponsored by the National Institute of Education, Russell, Mazzarella, White, and Maurer (1985) found that effective principals communicate clear goals for student performance and reinforce this with clear expectations for students' use of time. Teachers are expected to use the full period of time reserved for instruction. Less effective principals are less consistent. They speak of the importance of learning in vague terms, yet they communicate conflicting expectations and accept low performance standards. In extreme cases, they even allow students to schedule physical education for three of seven periods a day, hardly a compelling argument for the importance of academic learning time!

Where Expectations Are Communicated

According to our findings, effective principals take advantage of a variety of forums to project their expectations for teachers. Formal conferences with individuals and small groups, as well as general faculty meetings, are viewed as opportunities to reinforce goals. Pride in the school and its mission are common themes conveyed at student assemblies.

Formal gatherings are not the preferred situations for communicating expectations, however. More often, effective principals "drop in" during faculty committee meetings, planning periods, or between classes. Teachers often report that effective principals remind them of their purpose or preferred strategies during informal chats in the hallways. Informal meetings, particularly with individuals, are viewed as very effective opportunities for repeating and clarifying goals, as evidenced by the comments of this elementary school teacher:

> The principal frequently verbally reaffirms our school's goal to provide quality education for the underprivileged in our low-SES school. He is everywhere—in classrooms, cafeteria, playground—to insure that our students have every opportunity to benefit from their education. His constant emphasis focuses us all. Every staff member can tell the goal we have for the year. I know what's important and valued in our school. I plan accordingly.

Written communication is seen as another effective vehicle for stating expectations. Because newsletters inform in a public arena, they are used to relate selected goals and procedures. Private memos are chosen to inform individuals or groups of areas needing improvement.

The Power of Example

Can language alone influence teacher behavior? Imagine for a moment that you are the curator of a small art museum. You are in the process of selecting artists for an upcoming exhibit featuring the environment. Space is limited. I, as a freelance photographer, would like to persuade you to include my work in the exhibit. I tell you that black and white is my preferred medium, that I shoot only environmental subjects, and that I like to contrast the beauty of nature with the destructiveness of humankind. I ask you to "see" my work, but I cannot provide a portfolio. With words as my only form of persuasion, I have asked you to commit your resources and your reputation. If you are courteous, you will invite me to compete when I am more established. To yourself, you will scoff at my vanity!

Now let us suppose that a day later I return, portfolio in hand. You open the cover to reveal a single photograph. Your eyes are captivated by the graceful swan floating majestically on a crystal lake. I have used a technique known as "dodging" to lighten the swan's image, thus drawing your attention to this area. But after a moment, your eyes move to a darker image in the lower left corner. Almost hidden in the shadows, a second swan curiously pokes its beak into one of the six rings of a plastic soda pop holder. The contrast effectively invokes in you feelings of disgust and anger. Moved, you turn the page. There are no more photographs. I revert to verbal descriptions of forthcoming images. Based on a sample of one, are you now likely to "see" a place for me in your exhibition? How many more images must I produce to convince you?

Imagine now the vulnerable position of the new school principal. Expectations are clear; he or she repeats them over and over; he or she clarifies goals; messages are consistent. But what he or she wouldn't give for just one vivid photograph!

Our study reveals that teachers want and need examples of the behaviors they are expected to exhibit. Principals must rely to a large extent on the power of verbal persuasion, but effective principals provide examples to augment their verbal messages. The most effective example is the principal herself or himself.

Effective principals consistently model appropriate behavior. They place themselves on exhibit as a portfolio of one, an image for others to emulate. Because they expect teachers to provide a positive environment for learning, their attitudes are positive. Because they expect teachers to maximize learning time, they minimize disruptions by limiting visitors and announcements. Because they expect teachers to engage in professional development, they read and disseminate current educational research literature.

In addition to modeling, effective principals cite examples of specific behaviors that are consistent with their expectations. They not only expect teachers to use positive disciplinary methods, they also identify strategies from effective programs. One teacher ex-

plained how her principal tactfully persuaded her to send newsletters to parents:

> My principal uses ideas of what my peers are doing to
> influence me in the direction she wants me to go. For exam-
> ple, she likes for kindergarten teachers to send home news-
> letters. To get me started, she showed me examples of an-
> other teacher's letters. I started sending home newsletters
> immediately based on this incident. This strategy was a
> back-door, low intervention way of getting me to do what
> she valued.

Rather than dictate specific behaviors, the principal communicated expectations and showed examples. Thus, although
clearly influenced by the principal, the teacher was able to own
the solution:

> The principal wanted to have good home–school relation-
> ships. She used a strategy that allowed me to make the
> decision. She didn't make me send home newsletters. I
> chose to do this.

Guidelines for Effective
Use of Expectations

In conclusion, we have learned several lessons from our investiga-
tion of how effective principals use expectations to influence teachers. The following seven guidelines may assist the reader in developing appropriate strategies for communicating expectations that
positively influence teacher behaviors and attitudes.

1. Expect.

   First and foremost, effective principals do expect certain
   behaviors and attitudes of teachers. They see the result—the

whole exhibition—long before it is complete, and they expect teachers to complement the theme.

2. Communicate what is expected.

Effective principals use every available means—verbal and nonverbal—to communicate what is expected. They do not take for granted that all teachers share the same goals.

3. Communicate consistently.

Effective principals do not send mixed messages. A common theme is evident in their words and actions.

4. Repeat, restate, clarify.

Effective principals do not assume that a single utterance will be heeded by all. They understand the limitations to their own formal authority; they know the advantage of clarity, consistency, and redundancy in influencing teachers.

5. Seize and create opportunities.

Effective principals use all available forums for stating and clarifying their expectations. They take advantage of faculty meetings, student assemblies, newsletters, memos, and chance encounters.

6. Generalize expectations; personalize feedback.

Because effective principals are careful to communicate expectations consistently, their message is generally the same to all teachers (e.g., respect individual differences, discipline students positively). But because teachers react differently, the feedback they receive is personalized. Whether praising and rewarding or pointing out areas in need of improvement, principals should tailor feedback to the individual teacher. Thus, expectations may be expressed in a general faculty meeting, but suggestions for improvement are communicated privately, and rewards are tied to specific performance.

7. Provide appropriate models.

By modeling effective attitudes and practices, effective principals are their own best examples of desirable behavior. In addition, they provide specific examples of methods and programs congruent with their expectations. In sum, they become the first photograph in the exhibition, but they continuously describe the complete show while adding and inviting others to add pictures to support the theme.

References

Ackerman, R. H., Donaldson, G. A., & van der Bogert, R. (1996). *Making sense as a school leader: Persisting questions, creative opportunities.* San Francisco: Jossey-Bass.

Armor, D., Congry-Oseguera, P., Cox, M., King, N., McDonnell, L., Pascal, A., Pauly, E., & Zellman, G. (1976). *Analysis of the school-preferred reading program in selected Los Angeles minority schools.* Santa Monica, CA: RAND.

Austin, G. R. (1979, April). *An analysis of outlier schools and their distinguishing characteristics.* Paper presented at the annual meeting of the American Educational Research Association, San Francisco.

Blase, J., & Blase, J. (1998). *Handbook of instructional leadership: How really good principals promote teaching and learning.* Thousand Oaks, CA: Corwin.

Brookover, W. B., Beady, C., Flood, P., Schweitzer, J., & Wisenbaker, J. (1979). *School social systems and student achievement: Schools can make a difference.* New York: Praeger.

Dembo, M. H., & Gibson, S. (1985). Teachers' sense of efficacy: An important factor in school improvement. *Elementary School Journal, 86*(2), 173-184.

Edmonds, R. (1979). Effective schools for the urban poor. *Educational Leadership, 37*(1), 15-24.

Glenn, B., & McLean, T. (1981). *What works: An examination of effective schools for poor black children.* Cambridge, MA: Center for

Law and Education. (ERIC Document Reproduction Service No. ED 216 060)

Heck, R. H., Larsen, T. J., & Marcoulides, G. A. (1990). Instructional leadership and school achievement: Validation of a causal model. *Educational Administration Quarterly, 26*(2), 94-125.

Heck, R. H., & Marcoulides, G. A. (1993). Principal leader behaviors and student achievement. *NASSP Bulletin, 77*(553), 20-28.

Hipp, K. A., & Bredeson, P. V. (1995). Exploring connections between teacher efficacy and principals' leadership behavior. *Journal of School Leadership, 5*(2), 136-150.

Hoy, W. K., & Woolfolk, A. E. (1993). Teachers' sense of efficacy and the organizational health of schools. *Elementary School Journal, 93,* 356-372.

Kouzes, J. M., & Posner, B. Z. (1990). *The leadership challenge: How to get extraordinary things done in organizations.* San Francisco: Jossey-Bass.

Lasserre, C. (1989). *Relationships between selected school context variables and teacher self-efficacy and self-confidence.* Doctoral dissertation, University of New Orleans.

Lee, V., Dedick, R., & Smith, J. (1991). The effect of the social organization of schools on teachers' efficacy and satisfaction. *Sociology of Education, 64,* 190-208.

Purkey, S. C., & Smith, M. S. (1983). Effective schools: A review. *Elementary School Journal, 83*(4), 427-452.

Russell, J. S., Mazzarella, J. A., White, T., & Maurer, S. (1985). *Linking the behaviors and activities of secondary school principals to school effectiveness: A focus on effective and ineffective behaviors.* Eugene: University of Oregon, Center for Educational Policy and Management.

Rutter, M., Maugham, B., Mortimore, P., Ouston, J., & Smith, A. (1979). *Fifteen thousand hours: Secondary schools and their effects on children.* Cambridge, MA: Harvard University Press.

Sheppard, B. (1996). Exploring the transformational nature of instructional leadership. *Alberta Journal of Educational Research, 42*(4), 325-344.

Teddlie, C., Falkowski, C., Stringfield, S., Desselle, S., & Garvue, R. (1984). *Louisiana school effectiveness study: Phase two, 1982-84.* Baton Rouge: Louisiana State Department of Education Bureau of Research.

Tschannen-Moran, M., Hoy, A. W., & Hoy, W. K. (1998). Teacher efficacy: Its meaning and measure. *Review of Educational Research, 68*(2), 204-248.

Weil, M., Marshalek, B., Mitman, A., Murphy, J., Hallinger, P., & Pruyn, P. (1984, April). *Effective and typical schools: How different are they?* Paper presented at the annual meeting of the American Educational Research Association, New Orleans.

Influencing by Involving

Our principal is overt, informal, and extremely positive. He uses democratic procedures to make most decisions concerning our school. We have weekly leadership meetings for grade-level chairpersons so direct input comes from the teams. When something must be done in a particular manner, he very gently yet firmly requests our cooperation. Faculty meetings also are conducted in the same manner of openness and discussion, and group decisions are made. His entire manner and personality give his faculty the feeling of cooperation, togetherness, and mutual respect.

His goal is to provide an excellent education for our students in an atmosphere that is conducive to teachers' [positive] feelings and comfort. I feel that his approach to education is good and I want to copy it. I try to mirror his cooperative, friendly, positive attitude when dealing with students and parents. I feel that his approach is the best . . . and I know for a fact that he's the best principal in our county.

—An elementary school teacher

*I*n the preceding chapters, we discussed the strategies of praise and expectations used by open and effective principals to influence teachers. The use of these strategies gives teachers clear feedback regarding their principals' perceptions of their classroom performance and clear knowledge of the criteria against which principals judge success.

The next several chapters describe ways that principals increase teacher commitment and effort through careful attention to their professional needs. Specifically, we recount how principals described by the teachers in our study involved teachers in school-wide decisions, expanded teachers' autonomy in the areas of curriculum and instruction, and increased teachers' opportunities for professional development.

Shared decision making, empowerment, people-centering, involvement, teamwork, collaboration, participatory management, flat structures, shared governance—the terms are countless. Each year an organizational scholar adds a brighter bow, but the new packaging conceals old contents. Inside is the weapon proclaimed to fight bureaucratic inertia: participation by the workers in the governance of an organization (e.g., Conley & Bacharach, 1990; Glickman, 1993, 1998; Maeroff, 1988; Schlechty, 1990).

The rationale for school restructuring goes something like this: Each school serves a unique student clientele. Therefore, top-down governance, where goals and procedures are decreed for many different schools, is bound to fail. Teachers and school administrators, as professionals, are best qualified to make decisions affecting their unique student populations. Collective decisions that draw on the expertise of many teacher-professionals in a given school are superior to individual decisions made by an administrator.

What do other researchers report about the role of teacher participation as it relates to school effectiveness? A group of researchers comparing high- and low-achieving California schools concludes that governance of the school's instructional program has a direct effect on student achievement. Specifically, teachers in high-achieving schools are more involved in instructional programs than teachers in low-achieving schools. Principals in low-achieving schools are more likely to profess confidence in their teachers' abilities by "leaving them alone to teach" than by granting them participation in decision making (Heck, Larsen, & Marcoulides, 1990; Heck & Marcoulides, 1993; Riordan & da Costa, 1998).

Other researchers draw similar conclusions with regard to faculty participation in successfully restructured schools. Blase and Blase (1994) identify nine major strategies used by "exemplary" shared governance principals to enhance teacher empowerment and involvement in school-based decision making. Such strategies result in, for example, increases in teacher motivation, confidence, sense of ownership, reflection, commitment, risk taking, autonomy, and teaching efficacy. In another study, these researchers learned that similar effects on teachers result when principals considered to be effective instructional leaders use a range of "collaborative" strategies to influence classroom teaching and learning.

Another researcher found evidence of improved student achievement, lower dropout rates, gains in teachers' critical thinking skills, and improved school climate in Georgia schools that gave teachers a voice in school governance (Allen, Glickman, & Hensley, 1998; Glickman, 1990). These outcomes are attributed to the pride that developed as a result of teacher involvement and to a new manner in which teachers viewed their work.

Our teachers reported that open and effective principals encourage teacher participation in planning, choosing among alternative courses of action, and achieving agreed-on objectives. In fact, of all the influence strategies used by effective principals, teachers identified only one other strategy—praise—more often than faculty participation.

If I Have the Buck, Why Should You Get to Deal?

"The buck stops here." Harry Truman kept that reminder on his desk. In formal organizations, responsibility (and blame) rests with the person at the top of the hierarchy. Principals know that they are ultimately responsible for the outcomes of decisions made at their schools. (Very often, that message is reinforced by district supervisors.) So, if principals hold the buck, why should they allow teachers to deal the cards?[1] Our data underscore several reasons for "sharing the deal": Involvement in decision making by those affected by the decisions is used to create faculty unity, to improve morale, to engender support for decisions, and, perhaps most important, to improve the quality of decisions.

Faculty Cohesiveness and Morale

According to the teachers in our study, principals often express a desire to unite their faculties through collaboration. Language is used extensively to accomplish this goal; such words as *family, team, cooperation, community, unity,* and *harmony* are employed because they convey what effective principals hope to accomplish through participatory management. As one teacher commented, the principal involves teachers in group activities "to solidify the faculty's bonding to the school." Other principals express their interest in faculty unity through a variety of actions:

> He encourages everyone to take part in everything. Fundraisers, field day, or a faculty party/dinner—it doesn't matter. We are representatives of Lincoln Elementary. We all play or no one plays. We're a family of devoted people. We aim, plan, and succeed.

Closely related to the goal of faculty unity is the desire to improve teacher morale through inclusion. Participation is seen as a way to "diffuse problems that could demoralize faculty" by making "each teacher feel . . . part of the school family."

Fostering Support From Teachers

In our conversations with school administrators, we often hear the criticism that faculty empowerment reduces the power of the principal. In their version of "Why should I let them deal the cards," the skeptic and the politician argue, "After all, we were hired to run the school." Indeed, this argument is a salient one, particularly if a traditional management perspective prevails.

But power is not necessarily a finite resource. Our teachers disclosed that effective principals believe their power actually expands when it is shared. As one teacher explained, her principal seeks faculty input in decision making because "he wants ground-level support for his ideas. It's easier to support his agenda in a climate of trust and cooperation."

Kouzes and Posner (1990) concur with this view of power. In their study of the distribution of power in branch offices of a nationwide insurance company, they found that the leaders in the more successful branch offices understood, and acted on, [the belief] that "power is an expandable pie"—that power is not a zero-sum commodity, requiring that for others to have more, the leader must have less. The more everyone in the organization feels a sense of power and influence, the greater the ownership and investment they feel in the success of the organization. (p. 164)

The "expandability" of the power pie through shared ownership also was recognized by our teachers. Our research indicates that principals who want to ensure support (a "buy-in") for their policies and programs solicit teacher involvement at the early planning stages of a project, rather than mandating participation during the later stages of implementation.

Advantages of Shared Decision Making

Are decisions made by a group of teachers ultimately better decisions than those made by one or two administrators? From our data, we learned that the process of shared decision making significantly strengthens support for decisions and improves faculty morale. Still, the process is time-consuming and not without its detractors. Buck hoarding and power counting with finite numbers are not easily reversed. For administrators anxious about their own evaluations, the thought of relinquishing power while remaining unable to relinquish blame is a frightening proposition. The effective principals discussed in our study, however, recognized a decided advantage to shared governance: Shared decisions are usually better than individual ones.

Our teachers reported that their principals need teacher expertise to make informed decisions. Teachers' "formal and informal knowledge" (e.g., subject matter, expertise, and knowledge of student needs), "creative ideas," and "experience" all are valued by effective principals. Furthermore, we learned that task coverage (i.e., the number of tasks that could be accomplished) increases as a result of relying on others: "By diversifying decision making and tasks, the principal hopes to be more effective," one teacher explained.

In some cases, principals rely on teachers to compensate for their own areas of weakness. According to one teacher, "He [the principal] needs my organizing and verbal skills because he is insecure in these areas." Some readers might feel that delegation and participation are tools for less competent administrators who must cover their own shortcomings, but keep in mind that these were recognized as strategies used by open and very effective principals. Such school leaders apparently realize that they cannot provide effective leadership in all aspects of the school. At the Second International Congress on School Effectiveness, held in the Netherlands in 1989, Phil Hallinger argued that because of the multitude of leadership functions and the limited time available, principals (especially in high schools) should not attempt to centralize the role of instructional leader. Such restriction of involvement would reduce the likelihood of school effectiveness. Hallinger has urged principals to define the specific functions and behaviors of instructional leaders, to identify their own strengths in these areas, and to delegate functions outside of their expertise to a leadership team. Instead of viewing faculty participation and delegation as confessions of their ineptitude, effective principals should tout them as badges of their genius.

Teacher Effects

Attitudes Toward Involvement

Teachers in our study were excited about the opportunities offered by participatory school governance. Feelings of comfort, satisfaction, and heightened self-esteem were associated with increased involvement. When involvement took the form of participation in decision making, teachers felt especially valued and important: "I feel that what I think matters; I matter!" Teachers also felt more secure when formal structures for faculty input exist: "I feel that there is a way to channel ideas and concerns . . . there is a forum for my frustrations or trouble areas that arise."

Delegation of certain responsibilities, particularly extracurricular responsibilities, is another form of involvement that creates feelings of pride, inclusion, and empowerment for teachers. Terms such as *flattered, capable,* and *appreciated* were used to describe teachers' attitudes toward delegation. Teachers also developed a "whole-school perspective" or the ability to "see the big picture" as a result of their increased involvement. They reported becoming aware of the roles and responsibilities of others within the school and developing greater empathy for others as a result.

Indeed, the overwhelming response to being involved in the school in meaningful ways was quite positive; however, a few teachers mentioned occasional negative feelings. Additional demands on their time bothered some teachers, particularly when they felt that the issues being addressed were perceived as inconsequential: "Sometimes too much time is spent on minor details." The time problem as it relates to shared leadership should not be taken lightly. At the 1990 meeting of the American Educational Research Association, Carol Weiss revealed that in most of the schools she studied, teachers were used in an advisory capacity, and the overwhelming majority of issues addressed by school leadership teams were mundane and routine. These findings point to a basic truth: When teachers feel their time is being wasted on trivial matters, they are likely to resent involvement.

Closely related to the issue of time is the sincerity of principals who invite teachers to participate in school governance. If principals solicit teacher participation, teacher input must be reflected in the decisions ultimately made. Because faculty empowerment is such a popular notion in the school effectiveness literature, some administrators may obligingly implement superficial structures for shared decision making, with little intention of implementing decisions conflicting with their own preferences. They may limit faculty discretion to minor issues or they may engage teachers in time-consuming deliberations that tend to be ignored. To illustrate, one teacher in our study discussed feelings of manipulation in conjunction with her principal's use of faculty participation. Although the principal was evaluated as generally effective and his request for faculty input in key decisions was appreciated, the teacher resented his "tendency to do what he wants anyway" despite the input he received. Thus, faculty participation appears to be most effective when administrators learn to trust the decisions that ensue and when the issue at hand justifies the time expended.[2]

Given the difficulty in maintaining a focus on significant issues in restructured schools, Kirby's (1992) propositions are instructive with regard to effective practice:

1. Shared decision making will be more likely to address issues of greater significance when minor faculty concerns are resolved first, thereby fostering trust in the process and facilitating a more professional culture.

2. Shared decision making will be more likely to address issues of greater significance when teachers are able to focus their own work through formal structures for goal setting, determining agendas, and reaching decisions.

3. Shared decision making will be more likely to address issues of greater significance when teachers are involved in prioritizing concerns and when those teachers declare a stake in the outcomes.

4. Shared decision making will be more likely to address issues of greater significance when the database for generating concerns, alternatives, and solutions is both comprehensive and objective (such as an analysis of optimum and existing school effectiveness criteria to generate concerns or an Internet search to generate alternatives).

Involvement and Teacher Performance

In spite of the occasional misuses of faculty involvement, our teachers clearly were satisfied with its use. The attitudes of teachers are certainly important in determining the efficacy of any influence strategy, but of equal or greater importance are the effects on teacher behavior. Earlier we spoke of the goals that principals associate with the use of faculty involvement (e.g., faculty unity, improved morale, increased levels of support, better decisions). According to our data, teachers' reactions to increased participation are consistent with their principals' intentions.

Working Harder

Teachers reported that because of the availability of avenues for participation, time and energy increasingly were devoted to various aspects of decision making. While spending more time on planning and problem solving, teachers become more careful and self-reliant because they feel ownership in and responsibility for the school's effectiveness. One teacher explained, "I act cautiously in implementing and enforcing decisions because I know my principal's and my reputation are at stake." Another remarked, "I think more to look for a solution to a problem before asking for help. . . . I am a more capable person because I force myself to look at all angles before acting."

Many of the comments of teachers regarding participation implied dedication to the "team":

- ◆ "I know others depend on me to bring back information."
- ◆ "I am more willing to compromise when we don't agree."
- ◆ "I am supportive of ideas that develop through dialogue and will implement them whether I have been directly involved in the development of the task or not."
- ◆ "When you have a chance for input, you're not so quick to blame and point the finger."
- ◆ "If people give me responsibility, I feel compelled to carry it out well. I don't want to let others down."

Teachers attributed greater commitment, honesty, collegiality, and focus to their increased sense of belonging and being needed. They viewed faculty involvement as one of the most effective influence strategies. As one teacher summarized, "I am assured that what I do here matters . . . and often actually helps."

Returning From Abilene
(Or, Strategies for Involving)

In his whimsical parable "The Abilene Paradox," Jerry Harvey (1988) tells of his family's arduous journey in sweltering heat to eat dreadful food at a nameless cafeteria in Abilene, Texas. Why embark on such a journey? Because each member of the family thought that every other member wanted to go! Harvey blames such senselessness in groups on the failure to "manage agreement." Very often, he claims, members of formal or informal groups do what they believe others want. Everyone else is doing exactly the same thing. Because they fail to test their assumptions regarding agreement, groups often waste valuable time and energy doing things that no one really wants to do.

Likewise, there is often "mismanagement of agreement" on the benefits of increased involvement. Privately, the principal may say, "I'd like your input but you might think I'm shirking my responsibilities." To themselves, teachers may refrain, "We'd like more input but she might think that we're usurping her authority." Privately, everyone agrees, yet no one acts in accordance with their preferences. Harvey suggests that only through open and frank communication, initiated by one or more courageous individuals, can agreement be managed.

Although recognizing that agreement is a necessary first step toward increased participation, we also need to determine how we will work to achieve our purpose. Even if we agree to go somewhere, the road to Abilene may be fraught with potholes. Therefore, we offer a corollary to the problem of failing to recognize agreement. We agree with Harvey that organizational members often share the same goals without knowing it, but we also realize that goals and the strategies for achieving them are two separate issues, each offering possibilities for agreement or disagreement. Allow us to illustrate.

One author is reminded of a typical Saturday morning in July. Her children never understood the concept of "weekend." Rather than being able to relax and enjoy not having to go to school or camp, they wanted something to do. It was the middle of summer, and surely there were possibilities beyond watching Saturday morning cartoons and Mom mowing the lawn. Everyone agreed—the day was hot, all were bored, and they should find something to do. But that's where agreement ended. Attempting to "share" the decision, they found themselves inundated with strategies (even though there were only three people in this family)! The beach? One vote. A drive to the mountains? One taker. Fishing? One maybe, one yes, one no. Miniature golf? One definite no. . . . This give-and-take (or was it a give and give and give and give without any takers?) lasted most of the morning, frustrating everyone. Finally, all conceded that it was too late in the day to do anything.

This scenario will be familiar to many—husbands and wives, parents and children, a group of friends, a collection of teachers. We all have encountered situations in which we agreed that we wanted to do something but could not agree on what to do or how to do it. Similarly, school faculties and administrators often agree that they want to do something about increased involvement, but they have great difficulty reaching agreement on exactly what to do and how to achieve it.

We often ask students in our school leadership course to describe their concept of an empowered school. Because the majority of graduate students are practicing teachers and aspiring administrators, they are aware of the research supporting shared governance in schools. Most often (at least, in the safe setting of the university), agreement on this issue is managed without having to take the trip to Abilene. But our students are constantly amazed at the sheer number of issues that remain to be resolved even after they agree on the advantages of shared decision making. They grapple with questions such as:

◆ Who will be directly involved in making decisions—all teachers or a representative committee?

◆ If a representative committee is used, how will members be chosen? How long will they serve?

◆ What role will the principal and other administrators have in making decisions? Will they have an equal vote? No vote? Veto power?

◆ What issues are open to the process of shared decision making? Are any excluded?

◆ Who determines which issues will be addressed by the decision-making body?

◆ How are decisions ultimately reached? Majority vote? Consensus? Unanimous approval?

◆ Once decisions are made, who actually carries them out?

Not surprisingly, no two groups of students ever have created identical structures for faculty involvement. Many factors contribute to this: the proportion of teachers to administrators in the group, personal assumptions of group members (e.g., their views on power and authority), past experiences with shared governance, knowledge of possible governance structures gained through readings or training, and the level of creativity of the group. We should expect the same in actual schools. If schools are indeed idiosyncratic, it is unlikely that different schools would adopt the exact same structure for faculty involvement. In fact, Glickman (1990) cautions that one irony of empowerment is that "the more an empowered school becomes a model of success, the less the school becomes a practical model to be imitated by others" (p. 71). It seems that if a collection of individuals agrees to make decisions about where to go and how to get there, the individuals are obliged first to decide how they will decide. Using a decision made by any other group (i.e., adopting an existing model) negates the very first decision—agreeing to make decisions for themselves.

This rather lengthy introduction to involving others is intended as a cautionary note to those reading this chapter with hopes of answering the question "How can I effectively involve faculty in decision making?" The truth of the matter is that effective principals do it in many different ways. We offer the variations to be used, not in imitation, but in bits and pieces; to be pondered, remolded, and adapted wherever appropriate.

Formal Strategies for Involvement

Our data indicate that faculty involvement in decision making is most extensive when formal team structures are in place. Although the majority of principals who use involvement as an influence strategy do not themselves create such structures, those who do are perceived as more effective. Those principals tend to involve more people and to concede more authority on a wider range of issues.

We found that a variety of team structures are discussed and various designations are used—professional involvement committee, school climate committee, advisory council of teachers, and leadership management team.[3] Formal teams generally convene regularly, usually once a week. Team members are chosen most frequently on the basis of their roles in the school. Second-level administrators (e.g., department chairpersons, grade-level coordinators, counselors) seemed to make up most of the teams noted in our study. In some cases, teachers with no administration or coordination responsibilities also were included on the leadership teams.

Other staff members, such as cafeteria administrators, were involved occasionally.

Teachers who do not have opportunities to be on leadership teams tend to be involved in decisions on a more limited basis. They are expected to make suggestions to their team representatives either orally or in writing. In effect, their ideas could reach the team's agenda if activated through these channels.

For faculty members on leadership teams—either because of their other roles in the school or because of certain appointments or elections—involvement and effect are more direct. We found that teams usually assume a problem-identification/problem-solving orientation. Some teams focused almost entirely on problems identified by the principal, whereas others participated fully in identifying problems and developing solutions.

Teams address a broad range of problems. According to one teacher:

> All faculty members have the opportunity to give input by writing their concerns on a list posted on the "sign-in" counter in the office. No problem or concern is too small. Anything and everything listed on the agenda is discussed and answered.

Many of the teams noted in our study attempted to respond to any issue that cropped up and required attention. School climate, curriculum, student discipline, scheduling, faculty morale, parental involvement, fund raising, and student traffic control were among the many problems resolved by representative leadership teams.

Our data also suggest that formal authority for making decisions sometimes rests with the leadership teams. More often—in roughly 60% of the cases—teams served in an advisory capacity. According to one teacher, the principal "reserves decision making as an administrative prerogative; sometimes suggestions are implemented, other times they are not."

Informal and Impromptu Involving

Our teachers reported that informal participation opportunities also provide legitimate channels for them to express their thoughts and feelings on a range of personal and professional issues. Principals often endorse an open-door policy to encourage teachers to express their problems and concerns freely. Impromptu encounters with teachers are used to solicit input on a variety of problems. In addition, faculty meetings are conducted in a relaxed and open manner, allowing teachers the freedom to voice their concerns and to develop solutions collaboratively. Occasionally, faculty meetings are scheduled in response to problems that surface. In effect, teacher input is solicited during scheduled faculty meetings and during both scheduled and chance individual meetings.

Where no formal structure for faculty involvement exists, the faculty's role tends to be advisory only: Teachers give opinions, and principals make decisions. Nevertheless, teachers in our study were pleased that informal channels for participation allowed them input on many different issues.

Delegation is another informal involvement tactic used by open and effective principals. Whereas formal and informal meetings often are used for planning and generating alternative solutions to problems, delegation is used to inspire action. Here, principals are seen as extending varying degrees of authority and responsibility to teachers to resolve problems that surface or to handle extra-curricular activities. Teachers are selected for their expertise or for special qualities such as loyalty and pride. The selection of teachers by principals to assume added duties conveys confidence, which motivates teachers:

> My principal asked me to be in charge of organizing the work necessary for participation in the School of Excellence Program. Knowing the vast amount of writing that must be done, he chose me because I am an English teacher and a good organizer. I am flattered. I love a good challenge.

We should mention that the teachers who participated in the study on which this book is based have not been empowered fully. Although many teachers are involved in some capacity in the decisions made in their schools, few principals actually have relinquished a significant degree of authority. Still, teachers tell us that the involvement they have is preferable to none at all.

Suggestions for Effective Involvement

Again we must caution that a laundry list of do's and don'ts for effective involvement borders on hypocrisy. We cannot suggest the best team structure or the right distribution of authority or the most important activities to delegate; shared decision making means that the principal along with others must decide those issues. Other researchers found that establishment of a shared vision, consistent policies regarding delegation, risk taking, nurturing, and an educational rather than technical emphasis are mechanisms used by good principals to involve teachers (Rosenblum, Louis, & Rossmiller, 1994). From our research, we add these suggestions for facilitating faculty involvement.

1. Manage agreement.

    Before instituting formal or informal mechanisms for involving faculty in planning and decision making, principals must assess their own and their faculty's desire to undertake such an arrangement. The concepts of power and responsibility should be discussed openly; involvement will remain untried if lack of agreement is assumed. Change can begin when those involved in decision making risk discovering where agreement exists.

2. Involve individuals.

    Effective principals create a climate for participation by delegating responsibility to willing teachers who have the relevant knowledge and expertise.

3. Use every opportunity to involve informally.

    Effective principals involve others by inviting free expression of suggestions, advice, concerns, and problems. Among the available forums they use for soliciting teacher input are faculty meetings, chance encounters, and scheduled meetings with individuals or groups.

4. Encourage formal mechanisms for involvement.

Effective principals assist teachers in developing formal channels for faculty participation. When formal structures exist, teachers feel more involved and are more active in school governance.

5. Know when not to involve.

Effective principals increase faculty involvement because they expect positive results—perhaps improved morale, better decisions, or efficiency. If a decision that involves many people is expected to achieve the same or inferior outcomes as a decision made alone, the decision probably should be made alone. In the long run, teachers resent involvement on trivial matters. Such involvement will be seen as a waste of valuable time.

6. Respect the decisions of the team.

Regardless of the particular structure for faculty participation, effective principals value decisions that are made collectively. As such, they view themselves as members of the team—they are willing to share responsibility for dealing the cards and are willing to play the cards that are dealt.

Notes

1. The phrase *pass the buck* is believed to have originated in poker games, when a buckhorn-handled knife ("buck," for short) was used to designate the next player to deal a jackpot game.

2. We recognize that teachers also contribute to the success or failure of shared decision making. Weiss (1990) suggests that teachers themselves often choose to spend time on trivial issues because those issues are more familiar and less threatening. Development of teacher attitudes toward, and skill in, shared governance is certainly essential to its success.

3. For an overview of four models of shared governance in schools and the effectiveness of each in empowering teachers, see Hallinger and Richardson (1988).

References

Allen, L., Glickman, C., Hensley, F. (1998, April). *A search for account-ability: The League of Professional Schools.* Paper presented at the annual meeting of the American Educational Research Associa-tion, San Diego, CA.

Blase, J., & Blase, J. (1994). *Empowering teachers: What successful principals do.* Thousand Oaks, CA: Corwin.

Conley, S., & Bacharach, S. (1990, March). From school-site manage-ment to participatory school-site management. *Phi Delta Kap-pan, 71*(7), 539-544.

Glickman, C. D. (1990). Pushing school reform to a new edge: The seven ironies of school empowerment. *Phi Delta Kappan, 72*(1), 68-75.

Glickman, C. D. (1993). *Renewing America's schools: A guide for school-based action.* San Francisco: Jossey-Bass.

Glickman, C. D. (1998). *Education and democracy: The promise of Ameri-can schools.* San Francisco: Jossey-Bass.

Hallinger, P. (1989). Developing instructional leadership teams in high schools. In B. Creemers, T. Peters, & D. Reynolds (Eds.), *School efffectiveness and school improvement* (pp. 319-330). Am-sterdam: Swets & Zeitlinger.

Hallinger, P., & Richardson, D. (1988). Models of shared leader-ship: Evolving structures and relationships. *Urban Review, 20*(4), 229-245.

Harvey, J. B. (1988). The Abilene paradox: The management of agreement. In *The Abilene paradox and other meditations on man-agement* (pp. 13-36). San Diego, CA: University Associates.

Heck, R. H., & Marcoulides, G. A. (1993). Principal leader behaviors and student achievement. *NASSP Bulletin, 77*(553), 20-28.

Heck, R. H., Larsen, T. J., & Marcoulides, G. A. (1990). Instructional leadership and school achievement: Validation of a causal model. *Educational Administration Quarterly, 26*(2), 94-125.

Kirby, P. C. (1992). Shared decision making: Moving from concerns about restrooms to concerns about classrooms. *Journal of School Leadership, 2*, 330-344.

Kouzes, J. M., & Posner, B. Z. (1990). *The leadership challenge: How to get extraordinary things done in organizations.* San Francisco: Jossey-Bass.

Maeroff, G. I. (1988). Blueprint for empowering teachers. *Phi Delta Kappan, 69*(7), 473-477.

Riordan, G., & da Costa, J. L. (1998, April). *Leadership for effective teacher collaboration: Suggestions for principals and teacher leaders.* Paper presented at the annual meeting of the American Educational Research Association, San Diego, CA.

Rosenblum, S., Louis, K. S., & Rossmiller, R. A. (1994). School leadership and teacher quality of work life in restructuring schools. In J. Murphy & K. S. Louis (Eds.), *Reshaping the principalship: Insights from transformational reform efforts* (pp. 99-122). Thousand Oaks, CA: Corwin.

Schlechty, P. C. (1990). *Schools for the 21st century.* San Francisco: Jossey-Bass.

Weiss, C. (1990, April). *How much shared leadership is there in public high schools?* Paper presented at the annual meeting of the American Educational Research Association, Boston, MA.

Granting Professional Autonomy 5

The principal in my school supports his faculty and treats each member as a professional. He gives his teachers the freedom to teach without harassment. He is adept at hiring the kind of teacher who works well with students and other teachers. He then leaves the teaching to those who are trained, providing support when it's needed. I would find it demeaning and unsatisfying to work under the restraints imposed by many other principals. This man knows what to do to get the most from his teachers.

—An elementary school teacher

*W*ithin professional organizations, workers value autonomy in decision making. Colleagues serve as the reference group for evaluating choices, standards of control are self-imposed, and a professional code of ethics guides decisions. Within bureaucratic organizations, actions are judged against their conformity to rules, regulations, and expectations held by superiors. Conflict is inevitable when workers within bureaucratic structures see themselves as professionals and, therefore, demand autonomy (Hoy & Miskel, 1996). The bureaucratic emphasis on formal authority clashes with the professional valuing of expertise. Such conflict abounds in the bureaucratic structures of schools, where teachers demand professional recognition.

Autonomy refers to the degree of freedom that individuals have in determining work processes. By virtue of their expectations for professional status, teachers demand autonomy regarding curriculum and instructional decisions, particularly at the classroom level. Time use, resource allocation, methods of instruction, and procedures for student evaluation are some processes that teachers desire to control.

The formal position held by principals in school organizations is assumed by many to give them authority to influence behavior in schools. Teachers typically separate the educational function from the management function in acknowledging principals' authority, however. Teachers are willing to accept principals' authority in scheduling, public relations, and student services. In contrast, in the realm of instruction, teachers claim the authority of expertise and assert that this authority supersedes the principal's positional authority. This *authority paradox* (Donaldson, 1990) makes the instructional leadership role currently advocated in much of the school improvement and restructuring literature very difficult for school administrators to enact.

Hoy and Miskel (1996) assert that autonomy is undeniable in schools due to the physical isolation of teachers in their classrooms, the relatively infrequent opportunities for administrators to monitor teachers' work, and the broad authority teachers have over student activities. Although it may be true that autonomy at the classroom level is difficult to deny, there is great variability among schools in the amount of autonomy principals grant teachers regarding schoolwide issues. In one study of decision participation, it was found that teachers wanted more discretion in every decision area investigated, including school and classroom assignments, facilities planning, how and what to teach, and staff development (Bacharach, Bamberger, Conley, & Bauer, 1990).

Freedom From and Freedom To

Rosenholtz (1989) further distinguishes between two kinds of autonomy in schools: freedom *from* and freedom *to*. She found that where teacher commitment and collaboration are low, teachers are more concerned with freedom from. They are bored, helpless, and defensive. Constructing their own version of autonomy, teachers escape from such conditions with frequent absences. By contrast, teachers who are given frequent opportunities for learning and collaboration are more committed to their students and feel a freedom to grow and develop that has few limitations. Our teachers also alluded to both kinds of freedoms in their schools. They associated principal effectiveness with wide discretion in instruction and curriculum (i.e., freedom to) as well as with lack of intrusion and intervention (i.e., freedom from).

The Inspection Taboo

Rosenholtz (1989) refers to the desire of teachers in what she calls "stuck" schools to escape from the boredom and frustration of their everyday work conditions. Some teachers view this control as a form of power over their lives. In our study, we found that teachers associated freedom from close inspection with autonomy. They reasoned that because they are professionals, they are self-monitoring. Administrators, like office managers in a medical complex, are not to intrude in the professional realm. One teacher reported:

> [My principal] allows me to conduct my classroom as I see fit. He doesn't give unwanted advice and has never tried to "take over" my classroom . . . I think I do a better job as a result of not being hassled.

Meyer and Rowan (1977) argue that school administrators do avoid intrusion into the instructional realm. They attribute this avoidance to structural and psychological barriers rather than to their belief in the true professionalism of teachers. Because of the "loose coupling" (e.g., between teachers, subject areas, departments, and grade levels) characteristic of school organizations, teachers are afforded a high degree of autonomy. Allowing teachers to remain autonomous (i.e., not closely supervising them) gives the appearance of legitimating their professional status. Also, if principals supervise more closely, they risk uncovering defects in practice—defects that would require correction. Given that there is little certainty regarding what constitutes effective practice, principals are reluctant to confront teachers with accusations of ineffective practice. Thus, principals benefit from perpetuating what Meyer and Rowan call a "myth of professionalism." With increasing demands for accountability and instructional leadership in schools, it is not surprising that principals have denied that they purposely limit inspection of teachers (Okeafor & Teddlie, 1989). Nonetheless, teachers often associate avoidance with professional autonomy.

Our data suggest that the freedom from a dimension of autonomy is not an overarching concern of teachers who rate their principals as effective. These teachers, however, do convey an expectation that principals should intervene in their classroom practices only when asked and, in some cases, to assume a "very nonjudgmental, laissez-faire method of leadership." Likewise, Goldman, Dunlap, and Conley (1991) report that principals involved in one reform project saw their role not as interfering with teachers in their improvement efforts, but simply as helping them clear the way, particularly by making time available for teacher collaboration. More specifically, in studies of teacher empowerment and shared decision making, Blase and Blase (1994, 1997) found that successful principals encourage teacher autonomy by using strategies such as demonstrating trust, developing shared decision-making structures, encouraging innovation and risk taking, soliciting teachers' input, and buffering instructional time from interruptions.

Closer analysis of our data reveals, however, that teacher autonomy is significantly delimited. State and local policies and practices limit teacher discretion, but principals' expectations and advice also reduce teacher latitude in decision making. Although teachers associate autonomy with professionalism, they acknowledge limitations and the need for exceptions. Teachers stated:

- ◆ "She allows each teacher the freedom to teach within his/her own style, recognizing individual differences as long as we stay within the guidelines of the school philosophy."

- ◆ "He treats us as professionals . . . tells us the end results he expects . . . keeps us informed about what needs to be done . . . and leaves the many details to our discretion."

Thus, there did not seem to be an implicit assumption among these teachers that principals had no authority in the realm of instruction.

Teachers explained that because these principals were deemed effective on a number of dimensions, their advice and expectations were accepted. There is evidence that principals who demonstrate expertise in the areas of curriculum and instruction engender greater loyalty and satisfaction among teachers. Indeed, the amount of inspection and the limitations placed on work that is acceptable to teachers seem to be related to the professional respect that teachers hold for their principals' expertise. Freedom from may be of greater concern to teachers who work with less effective principals.

Autonomy: Freedom To

The most important aspect of autonomy for our teachers appears to be the freedom to teach in ways that teachers deem most effective. Teachers expressed strong convictions that they should be allowed to make decisions regarding what and how they teach. They reported that open and effective principals indeed grant them such authority:

◆ "I teach the information that I feel is more important."

◆ "I am at liberty to be an individual and use my own teaching techniques."

On the surface, granting autonomy seems to be a fairly straightforward technique: Teachers are left alone to make their own decisions regarding curriculum and instruction, at least within their own classrooms. Many teachers reported that principals modify autonomy in subtle ways, however. It is important to keep in mind that individual principals use many of the strategies reported in this book. Autonomy is nearly always used in conjunction with other strategies. Principals moderate their use of authority by conveying expectations for teacher performance. Further moderation results from the involvement of groups of teachers in schoolwide decisions. Although principals extend professional autonomy, groups of teachers—rather than individuals—are entrusted with critical decisions, as reported by teachers in our study. Finally, principals influence curriculum and instruction by disseminating information regarding effective teaching practices and by suggesting strategies for improvement. Ackerman, Donaldson, & van der Bogert (1996) argue further that responsibility for instructional supervision must be shared by teachers and principals alike. Following their suggestion, in the realm of curriculum and instruction, principals might increase teachers' collective autonomy by sharing accountability for teaching as a whole. Individual autonomy would be less valued. Support for teachers' involvement in the supervision of instruction is found also in a recent review of the knowledge base for school learning that concludes that emphasis on proximal variables such as curriculum and instruction has greater influence on student learning than emphasis on distal variables such as school-based decision making (Wang, Haertel, & Walberg, 1993).

Benefits of Changing the Myth to Reality

Whether professionalism in teaching is fact or myth, the benefits of treating teachers as professionals are indisputable. In spite of autonomy's somewhat tempered use, our study indicates that extending autonomy to teachers has overall positive effects on attitudes and performance. Teachers reported that autonomy makes them feel "proud," "professional," "confident," "competent," "trusted," and "free." Some disclosed that they became more reflective and creative in resolving classroom difficulties:

♦ "When I'm in a difficult situation . . . I can reflect on how a professional would handle it and follow through on my own."

♦ "I am encouraged and feel free to use my design and problem-solving skills."

Some teachers indicated that they conform to principals' expectations because principals respect their opinions and feelings. Others reported working harder and longer. Most felt that autonomy is deserved and essential:

♦ "A teacher doesn't need to feel timid about the use of their [sic] freedom and power."

♦ "I have the personality that does not like to be told what to do on issues that I see as my domain."

Only one teacher expressed some confusion resulting from the use of autonomy. His remarks demonstrate the mixed messages that can result when more direction from principals is desired. This suggests that the degree of autonomy granted must be appropriately matched to the ability and desire of the teacher:

> I feel gratitude and anger. I appreciate the opportunity to think about school improvement. I sometimes feel frustrated and angered by my isolation, lack of direction, and the assumption that I'll get it done.

Implications for Practice

We must take great caution in offering suggestions to use autonomy to influence teacher behavior. The term *autonomy* is interpreted differently in different settings and by different teachers. The degree of autonomy can range from absolute freedom and even laissez-faire behavior to limited discretion over defined issues in particular settings. Even when techniques are defined, the effects may vary from one teacher to another. Ever mindful of these constraints, we ask the reader to consider the following carefully.

1. Emphasize what is meant by autonomy. Emphasize freedom to, not freedom from.

   Be sure that teachers understand that they are given freedom to make decisions regarding curriculum and instruction. Explain whether that authority extends beyond the classroom. Insist that autonomy does not mean freedom from all forms of monitoring or supervision. In professional organizations, the autonomous are also accountable. (Of course, using Rosenholtz's, 1989, definition, there is an accompanying freedom from boredom and isolation.)

2. Emphasize that autonomy is extended out of a sense of professionalism and confidence. It is not an abdication of authority.

Some teachers resent the principal who fails to become involved in any capacity in decisions regarding instruction. By virtue of their expertise in pedagogy as well as administration, principals, too, can claim the status of professional educators. They should offer advice when asked and intervene when individual problems are detected. They should never equate teacher autonomy with laissez-faire leadership.

3. Use other influence strategies in conjunction with autonomy.

Granting professional autonomy alone is a very passive means of influencing teacher performance. Effective principals combine this strategy with other, more proactive, strategies— such as conveying expectations, involving groups of teachers in schoolwide decisions, providing professional literature related to improvement, and providing opportunities for professional development.

4. Assess individual readiness for autonomy.

Whereas some teachers are offended by overtly directive principals, others resent the nondirective or facilitative approach. For these teachers, and particularly for novices, feedback about performance should be frequent and semiprescriptive. The need for individual assistance should be assessed regularly through conferences with teachers and through informal classroom observations.

References

Ackerman, R. H., Donaldson, G. A., & van der Bogert, R. (1996). *Making sense as a school leader: Persisting questions, creative opportunities.* San Francisco: Jossey-Bass.

Bacharach, S. B., Bamberger, P., Conley, S. C., & Bauer, S. (1990). The dimensionality of decision participation in educational organizations. *Educational Administration Quarterly, 26,* 126-167.

Blase, J., & Blase, J. (1994). *Empowering teachers: What successful principals do.* Thousand Oaks, CA: Corwin.

Blase, J., & Blase, J. (1997). *The fire is back: Principals sharing school governance.* Thousand Oaks, CA: Corwin.

Donaldson, G. A., Jr. (1990, April). *Principals in transition: Dilemmas in moving from manager to instructional leader.* Paper presented at the annual meeting of the American Educational Research Association, Boston, MA.

Goldman, P., Dunlap, D., & Conley, D. T. (1991, April). *Administrative facilitation and site-based school reform projects.* Paper presented at the annual meeting of the American Educational Research Association, Chicago, IL.

Hoy, W. K., & Miskel, C. G. (1996). *Educational administration: Theory, research, and practice.* New York: McGraw-Hill.

Meyer, J. W., & Rowan, B. (1977). Institutionalized organizations: Formal structure as myth and ceremony. *American Journal of Sociology, 83,* 440-463.

Okeafor, K. R., & Teddlie, C. (1989). Organizational factors related to administrators' confidence in teachers. *Journal of Research and Development in Education, 22,* 28-36.

Rosenholtz, S. J. (1989). *Teachers' workplace: The social organization of schools.* New York: Longman.

Wang, M. C., Haertel, G. D., & Walberg, H. J. (1993). Toward a knowledge base for school learning. *Review of Educational Research, 63*(3), 249-294.

Leading by Standing Behind 6

A parent called my principal to complain that his child had been given a test that was different from the other students' tests. My principal then called me to his office, explained that a parent had made a complaint, and proceeded to gather details from me. . . . He was concerned about the rights of the parent, the student, and the teacher. He listened to each. . . . After I explained fully my method and reason for testing groups of students, he pointed out solutions as well as gave praise for my being a concerned teacher. The principal then called the parent and explained what we had discussed. The parent called back and asked the principal to thank me for what I was doing in the classroom.

—A middle school teacher

*I*n Chapter 4, we suggest specific techniques for involving teachers in setting school goals and the efficacy of those techniques in influencing teacher performance. Glickman, Gordon, and Ross-Gordon (1998) review theories of adult learning and motivation to inform their developmental approach to supervision of instruction. Within the context of the school, they contend, teacher development is enhanced by linking innovations to teachers' past experiences and providing teachers the time and support needed to learn about the innovation. These authors found that the "isolations, psychological dilemma, and lack of a shared technical culture" in schools mitigate against adult learning (p. 75). Interestingly, factors that we found to relate to adult learning also are related to improved student outcomes in a major synthesis of the best research on factors that increase student learning (Wang, Haertel, & Walberg, 1993). Open and effective principals in our study enhanced teacher capacity through direct assistance in four areas: provision of the material and financial resources necessary to teach, support for teachers in the area of student discipline, protection of allocated instructional time, and reward for teachers' efforts. In short, they are perceived as effective leaders because they understand that "leading" also means "standing behind."

Material and Financial Support

A critical component of leading by standing behind is the provision of fundamental resources. The careful selection and assignment of teachers to classes is unquestioningly a critical leadership function in effective schools, but the assignment of resources for teachers to perform their duties is equally important (Hord, 1988). Several independent research studies have associated the principal's resource-provider role with positive effects on classroom teaching and student learning (see, e.g., Ackerman, Donaldson, & van der Bogert, 1996; Andrews & Soder, 1987; Blase & Blase, 1994, 1997, 1998; Murphy & Louis, 1994). In spite of these findings, schools and teachers all too often are judged on the basis of student outcomes, with little regard for the differences in resources available to individual schools or teachers. Ironically, new teachers—those most in need of direct assistance—are often least likely to receive the raw materials necessary to teach (Kirby, Stringfield, Teddlie, & Wimpelberg, 1992).

Few schools offer teachers appreciable funds for the purchase of supplementary instructional materials or supplies. It is not uncommon for public school teachers to lack basic resources such as textbooks and paper. A graduate student lamented to one of the authors of this study that paper was strictly rationed at the middle school where he taught. He was allowed to make only 150 copies per week (exactly one page of paper per student!) in spite of the fact that weekly tests were encouraged and teachers were expected to send newsletters to parents on a regular basis.

Not surprisingly, our data suggest that open and effective principals recognize that improved teacher performance and professional growth are more likely to occur when basic materials are available. These principals ensure that teachers have ample textbooks, paper, and equipment to teach the required curriculum. Orientation sessions acquaint new teachers with available resources and encourage their use. Supplementary materials and financial support are used to encourage innovation. Because school improvement efforts often depend on new materials and training in new methods, more effective principals support the usual rhetoric for change with the tools and training to accomplish it. One teacher wrote:

> Time is a critical element in any school improvement effort. My principal provides me, and other teachers I work with, with almost unlimited "release" time to meet, plan, work out problems, and attend workshops. Even though half my work day is already dedicated to school improvement tasks, he is always more than willing to arrange for a substitute for my classes or those of my colleagues.

Teachers reported several positive consequences of receiving material and financial support for instruction and professional growth. They participated in a greater number of professional seminars and applied their new knowledge to the classroom. They reported feeling more "appreciated" and "encouraged" when given access to new resources, and were more reflective on how they used resources. Their support of school improvement programs increased; as one teacher stated, "With financial support I could see that I had access to the means of participation in improvement programs. It eliminated the old hang-up of enthusiasm [about the project] without means of accomplishment."

The specific kinds of resource support that teachers in the study associated with effective principals include tuition for conferences and seminars, substitute teachers to allow regular faculty to attend conferences, basic and supplemental instructional materials, and instructional improvement grants. In some cases, funds are allotted in response to teacher requests; however, many principals are more aggressive and anticipate teacher needs. Some are quite active in their pursuit of external resources:

> As a means to help the faculty achieve the schoolwide goal of increased student success, [my principal] and his assistant principals, with other staff members, applied for and won a $95,000 grant to be used to improve instructional techniques that would help students achieve greater success in the classroom. This was a deliberate effort to show that the principal would obtain the means by which the faculty could achieve its goal.

Support in Student Discipline

Early school-effectiveness research associated student achievement with an orderly and safe environment conducive to learning (Edmonds, 1979). More recent researchers have identified leader behaviors that enable a more studious atmosphere. Among these are high expectations for student achievement (Heck, Larsen, & Marcoulides, 1990; Heck & Marcoulides, 1993) and "backing up" teachers on matters of student discipline (Blase & Blase, 1994, 1998; Wang et al., 1993). We found principals' willingness to back up (or stand behind) teachers in their decisions regarding student misbehavior to be a powerful form of influence over teacher behaviors and attitudes.

Because classroom management is a frequent source of frustration for teachers, effective principals work to develop teachers' classroom management skills and support their decisions in disciplinary matters. Reasons why principals support teachers' discipline strategies go beyond desires to enhance morale, however. Teachers report that open and effective principals also recognize that support increases teachers' confidence ("[My principal] gives us the security to act on our own convictions"), which, in turn, increases their effectiveness in classroom management. These principals know that time expended on discipline reduces time available for instruction. Principals also seek reductions in classroom discipline problems to improve credibility with the public: "Well-behaved students create a positive image for the school."

Teachers told us, without exception, that principal support in matters of discipline results in feelings of "confidence," "security," and "control." The following excerpts from teachers' accounts reveal that these positive outcomes are attributed to the consistency and timeliness with which principals deal with discipline matters and to principals' support of teachers when conflicts arise with parents:

- ◆ "Students know exactly what is expected. Our principal's actions support his words."
- ◆ "He always listens to the problems you have with a student, then reacts immediately through some form of disciplinary action."
- ◆ "When being accused by a parent, I know I will be supported by [my principal] . . . Even though I may have done something wrong, I'm not belittled in front of a parent."

Teachers report working harder and accomplishing more in their classrooms because of the support they receive. Their classroom management skills improve as they adopt their principals' policy of clear expectations and consistent enforcement of rules:

- ◆ "He tells me to just tell students what is expected and then to hold them to that expectation . . . Stick to what I say, be firm, and I will gain their respect."
- ◆ "I am less willing to bend the rules."

Some teachers report developing more positive approaches to discipline:

- ◆ "I work more diligently to maintain discipline. I have come to think of this as an important part of education."
- ◆ "I spend more time seeking the positive side of each student."

Finally, and perhaps most important, teachers believe that they are more effective because discipline issues become less stressful:

♦ "I don't have to lose my temper when a child refuses to behave. I can go to the office for help."

♦ "I can do a more effective job if I don't have to tolerate disruptive students. I look forward to going to work."

How do open and effective principals support teachers' discipline efforts? In our study, support apparently began with the development of a formal schoolwide discipline program. Principals collaborated with teachers to develop and implement fair and consistent policies. Some principals provided time for teachers to participate in assertive discipline programs. The effects of such approaches are obvious in the remarks of this teacher:

> One of the strategies which has been emphasized at our elementary school is the assertive discipline approach. This approach allows the teacher to be assertive and positive . . . With the type of students our school has, this strategy has proven to be very effective because our students are conditioned to hearing unpleasant remarks about themselves . . . This strategy allows me to be positive. I feel like I have been changed as a teacher.

On an individual basis, principals assist teachers with student discipline by listening, giving advice, and solving problems. They constantly stress the need for clear expectations for student conduct and for consistency and fairness when dealing with disruptive students. When conflicts arise with parents, principals publicly support their teachers and help to solve problems. One principal has a policy of allowing teachers to bring parents to her office to finish conferences that appear to be getting out of control. Although a teacher reported that she had to take only one parent to the principal's office, she appreciated "the security of the principal's assistance . . . in these difficult situations." More indirectly, principals support teachers by their visibility in the school, particularly in the hallways.

Protecting Instructional Time

Safire and Safir (1990) tell the story of Charlie Grimm, coach of the unsuccessful Chicago Cubs in the 1930s and 1940s. Approached by an excited recruiter who had just seen a pitcher strike out 27 batters, allowing only one foul, Grimm rejected the young recruiter's desire to extend an attractive offer to the pitcher. Instead, he instructed, "Sign up the guy who got the foul. We're looking for hitters" (p. 14).

Similarly, our data indicate that effective principals understand that the key to improving their schools' effectiveness lies not with persons skilled in compliance with bureaucratic rules and procedures or in discussions about those rules, but in effective use of time allocated for instruction. In spite of pressures to maintain records and meet reporting deadlines, they recognize that what they need are teachers, not bureaucrats. Thus, a third strategy used by open and effective principals to increase instructional time and improve teacher morale is the deliberate reduction of extraneous demands on teachers' time. They give teachers time to teach.

Principals deemed effective in our study are aggressive in reducing interferences for teachers in two areas: paperwork and meetings. Compliance with state and federal standards has greatly increased the amount of paperwork required in schools over the last two decades. Teachers, frustrated by the additional demands on their time, are most responsive to principals who engage in actions to limit paperwork. Although the principals are unable to eliminate paperwork entirely, teachers express appreciation at their principals' concern:

> An abundance of paperwork is causing teacher burnout, stress, and negative attitudes toward our profession. Our principal (whenever possible) tries to reduce the amount of paperwork we must do. I appreciate this and try to do my job as best I can.

The principals also reinforce the value they place on instructional and planning time by limiting the number of faculty meetings. Whenever possible, they conduct informal meetings with individuals or small groups rather than with the whole faculty.

Attempts to reduce interference have a positive effect on teacher attitude, which is linked to teacher performance. One teacher noted that she is more effective because she feels more relaxed: "I don't feel pressured or under stress. I am able to work harder and get the job done."

Protection of instructional time has been found to be an important form of influence on teacher behavior in other studies as well (see, e.g., Heck et al., 1990; Heck & Marcoulides, 1993). Joyce and Showers (1995) found, however, that teacher innovation is possible only when teachers who try new practices are released from competing demands on their time. With regard to meetings, Hord (1988) warns that what teachers need is "more time for instruction and less for 'instructions' " (p. 9). Hord (1997) found that valuing and protecting instructional time is a key element of principals' leadership behavior in professional learning communities.

Tangible Incentives

In 1983, David Parks wrote,

> One of the most perplexing problems facing educational leaders in a period of austerity is how to maintain the cooperation and performance of a group of demoralized professionals. How does one compensate professionals for inadequate books and supplies, large classes, disruptive students, public criticism, limited assistance, increased duties, and the lowest salaries paid to highly educated personnel in the nation? How does one lead a group in which morale is so low that over 40% of survey respondents would not again select teaching as a profession and 57% are definitely planning to leave, will leave if something better comes along, or are undecided about staying? (p. 11)

Parks offers several recommendations for motivating teachers in times of austerity. A more attractive work environment and intangible rewards such as recognition are among his prescriptions.

Nevertheless, he cautions that such intangibles could serve only as temporary substitutes for tangible rewards.

We found that even in times of austerity, many principals bolster teachers' spirits by providing tangible rewards. Although the goals associated with such rewards are sometimes performance related, more often principals use rewards to improve morale and reduce absenteeism. Thus, unlike praise, which is usually tied to specific accomplishments, principals reward teachers by celebrating events such as holidays, birthdays, homecoming, and in-service days.

Some leadership theories suggest that extra effort or extraordinary performance is unrelated to such extrinsic rewards, but they recognize that ordinary performance and satisfaction are connected to the stipulations of the work contract (see, e.g., Bass, 1990). Performance—at least at some minimal level—is given in exchange for tangible rewards.

With only one exception, we found that teachers were motivated by tangible incentives. Teachers even claimed that rewards encourage innovation and extra effort beyond the confines of the classroom. Some teachers reported that they work specifically to achieve awards. Only one teacher expressed negative feelings about her principal's use of tangible incentives: "He does not believe that I as a professional will come to work because of internal motivation. I resent that." For some readers, the use of rewards may seem patronizing. The sincerity and genuineness of the principal may be essential to the acceptability of the strategy. Principals who use tangible incentives may positively influence teachers because they are also honest, caring, and nonmanipulative. As one teacher whose remarks more closely approximate the majority view pointed out: "[Rewards] show us that the principal cares."

Because educators appear to be "stuck" in austerity, it is not surprising that tangible incentives dispensed by principals were of little monetary significance to the teachers in our study. Food was the most frequently discussed incentive. Some principals serve coffee and doughnuts at staff meetings; others order breakfast or lunch for teachers on in-service days. One teacher reported that her principal cooked a steak dinner for the whole faculty. Buttons, pins, and ribbons are used to recognize teachers on special occasions. Shirts with school logos are awarded for special accomplishments. Corsages are presented to teachers at homecoming events.

Some principals sponsor social events to build morale. These goes beyond the usual office Christmas party; one more creative principal, for example, holds an ice cream party on St. Patrick's Day. Occasionally, principals compensate for their inability to dispense monetary rewards by giving certificates entitling teachers to arrive late or leave early. These are tied to specific accomplishments such as perfect attendance, for which some teachers are given half-day-off certificates.

How to Lead
by Standing Behind

Based on the reports of our teachers, it appears that effective principals are quite creative and aggressive in standing behind their teachers. Principals support their schools' instructional goals by serving as resource providers and guardians of instructional time. They assist teachers with student discipline matters, allow teachers to develop discipline codes, and support teachers' authority in enforcing policy. Even when teachers err, they are allowed to "save face" before parents and students. Also in recognition of teachers' professionalism, open and effective principals are creative in making the workplace more attractive to teachers by sponsoring special events in their honor. The following lessons are gleaned from the many forms of support noted by the teachers in our study.

1. Devote ample time to orient new teachers to school and district resources, including print and film media, equipment, textbooks, and supplies.

   Explain policies for use of equipment and encourage teachers to seek assistance when needed. If supplies are rationed, explain the rationale as well as the policy. Remember that the novice has not had time to build a personal library of resources; provide access to catalogs and funds for the purchase of supplemental materials.

2. Ensure that all teachers have a sufficient number of appropriate textbooks and materials for all students.

Check resources before school begins and periodically solicit input from teachers regarding appropriateness and adequacy. Do not make demands that teachers cannot meet because of limited resources.

3. Provide the means for teachers to attend professional development conferences.

Whenever possible, tuition to conferences should be paid for teachers, and substitutes should be provided to cover classes missed. Astute principals keep informed of professional development opportunities for teachers and encourage participation. All reasonable requests for teachers to attend conferences and seminars should be entertained.

4. Collaborate with teachers to write school improvement grants.

Rather than lament the inadequacy of funds necessary to produce meaningful educational change, aggressive principals seek alternative sources of funding from business partnerships and federal, state, and local grants.

5. Work with teachers to develop and implement a schoolwide student discipline policy.

Ensure that a clearly written policy exists for addressing problems of student conduct. When violations occur, enforce the policy consistently and in a timely manner.

6. Support teachers' decisions on discipline issues unless those decisions are inconsistent with written policy.

In spite of formalized procedures, some cases will require subjective judgment. Unless the teacher's decision is inconsistent with written policy or unfair to the student, support the teacher's authority. If it becomes necessary to rule against the teacher, carefully explain the decision in private.

7. Monitor and develop teachers' classroom management skills.

Many teachers leave the profession in the early years because they never learn to manage student discipline. Assure that every teacher has a reasonable opportunity to develop proficiency in instruction by providing assistance in classroom management.

8. Take time to listen to teachers who have problems with student discipline.

In many cases, empathy is all that teachers need to resolve their own student discipline problems. Give them the time to voice their concerns, listening carefully for signs that corrective measures are warranted and offering assistance if desired.

9. Limit the number of scheduled meetings.

Effective principals covet planning and instructional time. Whole faculty meetings are kept to a minimum. Memos and small group meetings often serve the same needs.

10. Limit paperwork.

Teacher aides and secretarial staff should be used to limit the amount of teacher time required for paperwork. To the extent possible, reporting functions should be centralized.

11. Provide creative tangible rewards.

In a much-criticized and underpaid profession, small rewards greatly improve morale. Seize every opportunity to brighten teachers' work lives with visible signs of appreciation, such as small gifts, release time, or periodic refreshments.

References

Ackerman, R. H., Donaldson, G. A., & van der Bogert, R. (1996). *Making sense as a school leader: Persisting questions, creative opportunities.* San Francisco: Jossey-Bass.

Andrews, R. L., & Soder, R. (1987). Principal instructional leadership and school achievement. *Instructional Leadership, 44,* 9-11.

Bass, B. M. (1990). *Bass and Stogdill's handbook of leadership: Theory, research, and managerial applications* (2nd ed.). New York: Free Press.

Blase, J., & Blase, J. (1994). *Empowering teachers: What successful principals do.* Thousand Oaks, CA: Corwin.

Blase, J., & Blase, J. (1997). *The fire is back: Principals sharing school governance.* Thousand Oaks, CA: Corwin.

Blase, J., & Blase, J. (1998). *Handbook of instructional leadership: How really good principals promote teaching and learning.* Thousand Oaks, CA: Corwin.

Edmonds, R. (1979). Effective schools for the urban poor. *Educational Leadership, 37*(1), 15-24.

Glickman, C. D., Gordon, S. P., & Ross-Gordon, J. M. (1998). *Supervision of instruction: A developmental approach* (4th ed.). Boston: Allyn & Bacon.

Heck, R. H., Larsen, T. J., & Marcoulides, G. A. (1990). Instructional leadership and school achievement: Validation of a causal model. *Educational Administration Quarterly, 26*(2), 94-125.

Heck, R. H., & Marcoulides, G. A. (1993). Principal leader behaviors and student achievement. *NASSP Bulletin, 77*(553), 20-28.

Hord, S. M. (1988). The principal as teacher educator. *Journal of Teacher Education, 39*(3), 8-12.

Hord, S. M. (1997). *Professional learning communities: Communities of continuous inquiry and improvement.* Austin, TX: Southwest Educational Development Laboratory.

Joyce, B. & Showers, B. (1995). *Student achievement through staff development: Fundamentals of school renewal* (2nd ed.). White Plains, NY: Longman.

Kirby, P. C., Stringfield, S., Teddlie, C., & Wimpelberg, R. (1992). School effects on teacher socialization. *International Journal of School Effectiveness and Improvement, 4,* 187-203.

Murphy, J., & Louis, K. S. (1994). *Reshaping the principalship: Insights from transformational reform efforts.*. Thousand Oaks, CA: Corwin.

Parks, D. J. (1983). Leadership in times of austerity. *Educational Leadership, 40*(5), 11-13.

Safire, W., & Safir, L. (1990). *Leadership.* New York: Simon & Schuster.

Wang, M. C., Haertel, G. D., & Walberg, H. J. (1993). Toward a knowledge base for school learning. *Review of Educational Research, 63*(3), 249-294.

Gentle Nudges:

Suggesting Versus Directing

7

Our principal was able to influence us to develop our curriculum thoroughly. Through the force of his leadership, we generated course goals and behavioral objectives, care- fully linked them to an articulated curriculum, and devel- oped an integrated scope and sequence for our content area in grades 7 through 9. This was a new area for all of us at the time and it was not something we did willingly. [He] didn't force us to do this work. He carefully, logically, and gently laid out the research on the importance of this kind of cur- riculum development and then paid us to write it. He was flexible about the hours we worked and the amount of time we spent at lunch. He would stop by as we worked, always seeming interested in our work—not checking up on us.

—A middle school teacher

Several of the strategies discussed in earlier chapters, such as praise and rewards, are used by effective principals to improve teacher morale. Others, such as involvement and expectations, are used to improve teacher commitment. Some, such as providing adequate resources, ensure that teachers are able to perform effectively.

Many of the strategies discussed thus far indirectly affect classroom instruction. Teachers who are more involved in schoolwide decisions, for example, report being more innovative; those whose efforts are acknowledged report being revitalized. Other strategies, however, are intended to improve instruction more directly.

Because administrative authority in the realm of instruction is limited by teachers' desires for professionalism and autonomy, strategies used by principals to improve instruction must be used with considerable diplomacy. Principals must demonstrate respect for teachers' choices and acceptance of multiple teaching styles and strategies. Their help must be perceived by teachers not as orders, but as friendly, concerned advice. For this reason, we refer to this group of strategies as "gentle nudges." Similarly, Allen, Glickman, and Hensley (1998) found that 66% of the principals they studied had come to view their role as that of encourager, supporter, or enabler. Gentle nudges took several forms in our study; the most frequent were related to providing teachers with professional literature, training opportunities, and suggestions.

Appropriate Intervention

Although effective principals typically use indirect methods of intervention, such as advice, in some cases they simply tell teachers what to do or act on teachers' behalf. These occasions include crisis situations and requests for help.

We found that principals use direct intervention primarily in response to teacher requests. When their help was requested, the principals described by teachers in our study were likely to intercede quickly and report back to the teacher initiating the request.

The principal's assistance with a range of problems—instructional and noninstructional in nature—was solicited by teachers in the study. For example, a female teacher reported being sexually harassed by another teacher. When notified, her principal immediately took control of the situation: "She listened . . . told me exactly what she was going to do . . . and asked me later if there was still a problem." In addition to resolution of the immediate problem, increased teacher respect for the principal was a direct outcome of this encounter. The teacher was relieved and appreciative that "[the principal] did not treat me as though I was crazy or as though I asked for it."

In crisis situations, effective principals also use direct intervention to affect teachers' performance. In these cases, the urgency of the situation requires that the principal give orders rather than suggest strategies. Principals use directives to prevent further escalation of crises. They explain situations to their teachers, anticipate possible consequences, and give specific directions for dealing with those consequences.

Principals who use direct intervention in crises are successful in limiting loss and containing disorder. Teachers expressed relief at being told how to act under stressful circumstances:

> When a student committed suicide [the principal] held a morning faculty meeting in which he communicated all the information we needed . . . how to address students . . . "what if" types of situations we might be confronted with. . . . I was able to comfort, answer questions, send the students who needed special help to the appropriate source, and handle the situation professionally.

Have You Considered . . . ?

Under more typical circumstances, effective principals use fewer directives; instead, they influence teachers through advice or suggestion. Effective principals studied by Blumberg (1989) were quite candid about their use of suggestion. Understanding that curriculum and instruction were the "territorial prerogatives" (p. 144) of teachers, these principals planted suggestions for consideration rather than intruding into teachers' domain. Blumberg refers to this technique as "seeding." Principals consider all possible alternatives to an instructional problem and select those that are acceptable, then present only those to teachers. Thus, they inform teachers of the alternatives they prefer, but soften their involvement by allowing teachers to control final choices about matters in their professional realm. In a recent study of teachers, Blase and Blase (1998) confirm the importance of suggestions in influencing and motivating classroom behavior.

Teachers in our study also reported that principals motivate them to examine alternative instructional methods by relying on interpersonal diplomacy and informal conversation. When teachers ask for help with an instructional matter or when a problem is perceived by the principal, these principals present options for teacher consideration. Rather than require teachers to correct their deficits in a prescribed manner, principals allow teachers to make choices from among alternatives. As one teacher reported:

> [My principal] will ask for my opinion on how to do things and then offer suggestions. . . . He may ask if I considered trying a particular way of doing a task. . . . I tend to be open to his suggestions and willing to give consideration to his ideas.

As a result, some teachers disclosed that they became more reflective about their own decisions. Some responded selectively to their principals' suggestions. As one teacher noted, "I have begun to use some ideas in formulating my own theories rather than accept something she says." In most cases, teachers reported accepting or trying some aspect of the principal's advice.

The language used by principals to offer ideas for improvement reflects the fragile, tenuous nature of the authority relationship between principal and teacher in the area of curriculum and instruction. Principals deemphasize their power by suggesting rather than directing, but further deemphasis is noted in the presentation of suggestions. Principals usually do not portend to know the best course of action. Instead, they present advice through questions, such as "Have you considered . . . ?" or "What if you tried . . . ?" One principal was described as follows:

> [He's] not the type to directly tell you to do something. This is very good because it creates a positive atmosphere. . . . He believes his teachers should have input on every area of our school. . . . When we discuss discipline, he uses questioning as a means of influence . . . a question such as "don't you think . . . ?"

In response to this indirect and nonthreatening mode of instructional supervision, teachers reported feeling "relieved," "relaxed," and "free." Professional autonomy is a direct outcome: "I am given the benefit of making the decision on my own." Direct effects on performance were noted in nearly every case:

◆ "I will give things a try because I do not feel threatened if they fail."

◆ "I try to conform to what I feel she wants."

◆ "I try to do a better job . . . work harder to make a unit more successful."

Power in Empowering

Faculty empowerment is often narrowly construed as participation in decision making. Maeroff (1988), an early empowerment theorist, argues that empowerment requires elevating teachers in terms of status and knowledge as well as giving them access to schoolwide decision making. He views staff development as an appropriate vehicle for increasing teacher status and knowledge. Recent works of others strongly support Maeroff's argument (Blase & Blase, 1994, 1997; Clift, Johnson, Holland, & Veal, 1992; Short & Rinehart, 1992).

Administrators are realizing more and more that empowering teachers requires more than providing opportunities to act to achieve school goals. Decision participation alone may not increase teachers' power to improve schools. Of equal importance (and perhaps this is a prerequisite) is helping to develop the ability to act, which is achieved through enhancement of teachers' knowledge. Teachers must be provided opportunities to acquire the knowledge necessary to warrant classroom autonomy and authority over schoolwide decisions (Kirby, 1992). As Hawley (1988) cautions, the ability of restructured schools (of which faculty empowerment is a critical component) to improve student achievement is "conditioned by the collective competence levels of the teachers involved" (p. 427). Unfortunately, empowered faculties often rely on their existing repertoire of skills and knowledge rather than availing themselves of opportunities to build on that base (Weiss, 1990).

Our study indicates that effective principals do not accept teacher skill and knowledge as bounded by past learning. In addition to suggesting techniques for instructional improvement, effective principals use two other subtle strategies to increase teachers' knowledge: They create opportunities for professional development and they provide teachers with current professional literature.

Professional Development

Principals provided teachers in our study with both formal and informal opportunities to develop practical knowledge and skills. Informally, the principals made themselves available to assist teachers as needed. They often provided assistance in areas of special interest; several principals, for example, assisted teachers with computer use for instructional and record-keeping purposes.

Among the other topics of particular interest to the principals were drug use, divorce, death, and child abuse. Formal training sessions, often conducted by outside experts, provided teachers with information about these topics. Staff development in curriculum and in instruction issues, such as language methods and questioning strategies, also was provided.

Perhaps as important as the specific topics chosen for staff development is the discretion afforded teachers in selecting which components to implement and which to ignore. The teachers felt that they could reflect on newly acquired information and choose those pieces most beneficial to them and their students:

> The principal is a big advocate of whole language instruction, and, as a school goal last year, did whatever she could to make sure the implementation of the program flowed smoothly. Teachers were trained throughout the previous year. They were not mandated to implement the program, but were encouraged to implement the parts that they were comfortable with. I guess she trusted us and let us go at it! I felt so comfortable in the school, implementing parts of the program. I had the freedom to be creative, and my children benefited most.

The behavioral and affective outcomes that the teachers associate with training are quite positive. They reported feeling "confident" and "appreciative." Their awareness of important issues—

such as the role of expectations in student performance or the process and purpose of empowerment—increased. Changes in teacher behavior were generally consistent with the purposes of training. For example, computer training sessions tended to increase teachers' use of computers in the classroom. New discipline and instructional techniques were practiced, albeit with some selectivity.

Two factors explain the effectiveness of this strategy in affecting teacher performance. As mentioned earlier, discretion in implementing new learning allows teachers to retain control over decisions affecting their classrooms. Additionally, pragmatism is used to explain the effectiveness of training. For many teachers, knowing that "the children benefit from it . . . makes it worthwhile."

Professional Literature

A final strategy used by open and effective principals to influence instruction is providing teachers with professional literature. Unfortunately, many educators tend to limit their search for assistance to other teachers in the same building. This may further compound the isolation that characterizes teaching and also may restrict opportunities for creative and current improvement options.

Researchers have learned that principals in highly collaborative professional cultures encourage many forms of staff development, including training and dissemination of professional literature (Blase & Blase, 1998; Leithwood, 1994; Leithwood & Jantzi, 1990). Authors note that staff development acknowledges that one's own colleagues, as well as external experts, possess useful information for guiding school improvement efforts. This awareness fosters collaboration, which in turn fosters a desire for further growth. Thus, the principal who promotes faculty growth and involvement will provide resources and opportunities for development.

The effective principals discussed by teachers in our study kept abreast of trends in instruction and curriculum, informed teachers of these advancements, and encouraged them to try new techniques. By doing so, they were able to expand teachers' abilities to improve instruction and to support their beliefs that improvement is possible with attention to empirical evidence documented by others.

Teachers also explained that effective principals distribute articles from research and professional journals, magazines, and newspapers. In most cases, these are related to effective teaching or effective schools' practices. Curriculum writing, discipline techniques, and computer use also are covered, but less frequently. In essence, their principals use the gentle nudging approach, placing literature in teachers' mailboxes with little or no further comment:

> The principal of our school is interested in improvement of instruction which he verbalizes in faculty meetings and in informal school settings. He relates research and theories in small-talk situations. He also places in our mailboxes little thought-provoking ideas concerning teaching effectiveness. . . . People tend to read and discuss much of the effectiveness tidbits.

Some principals are very explicit about their expectations for the use of professional literature. One principal told teachers that they were to read the materials and then provided time for them to discuss the content. During this time they were also to plan how they would apply the information. Other principals were less directive.

From the teachers' perspective, dissemination of professional literature enhances their awareness and motivation to improve. Consider these pragmatic and open-minded attitudes expressed by teachers:

♦ "I feel like I'm at least somewhat current on key issues in education . . . I reassess my attitudes after reading the articles."

♦ "It makes me more interested in various educational strategies and motivates me to improve on my own . . . I can try if I want."

The latter comment emphasizes again the importance of allowing teachers choice about whether or not to implement the strategies they have read about. This may account for the very positive attitude the majority of teachers took toward this influence strategy.

One more skeptical teacher noted that "it would take a lot more time, money, and effort to dramatically change teachers' methods of doing things after they have been ingrained over several years." As Leithwood and his associates note (Leithwood, 1994; Leithwood & Jantzi, 1990; Leithwood, Tomlinson, & Genge, 1996), teachers are much more open to growth opportunities such as professional literature when a strong commitment to school improvement goals exists. The interactive nature of professional development, goal commitment, and work collaboration deserves considerable attention by those attempting to influence teacher growth. The reader should keep in mind that none of these strategies is used in isolation. Furthermore, although teachers rate each strategy as highly effective in influencing their performance, they judge their principals in general to be open and effective on the basis of their overall approach, not on the basis of any one strategy. Effective principals who work to enhance professional growth undoubtedly also build faculty involvement.

A second caution is also in order regarding the use of professional literature. Overall teaching is positively influenced by this strategy. Some try new instructional techniques: "I try more ideas and techniques . . . I believe I have increased my effectiveness." Classroom demeanor is affected as well. A teacher who had been given some literature on the effects of teacher attitude toward students remarked, "I changed my actions. For example, this fall I made an effort to be gracious in welcoming new students to my already overcrowded classroom." Our data suggest that long-lasting effects of the use of professional literature are not guaranteed, however. A teacher describing what occurred in her school commented that "most teachers, including myself, used the methods for a while and then got bogged down with the details." This suggests a need to follow dissemination of materials with encouragement and monitoring regarding implementation as well as follow-up help, if needed.

Overall, teachers rated the use of professional literature as quite effective in influencing their classroom behavior. Their explanations for effectiveness shed some light on how the strategy can best be used. First, principals were careful not to overload teachers with complex or abundant materials. One teacher commented that "the ideas are simple teaching or management ideas that can be easily incorporated into lessons. Given just one idea now and then it's not overwhelming and more apt to be tried." A second justification was the emphasis on teacher discretion, which was equated with professional respect: "[The principal] gave us freedom as we worked. He valued us as professionals." Finally, respect for the principal made this an acceptable strategy for many teachers: "I have great respect for her . . . and feel that her judgments are worth my efforts."

On Nudging and Intruding

Our data suggest that effective principals know when it is appropriate to intrude into teachers' work space and when it is advantageous to tread more cautiously. During crisis situations, when immediate action is necessary to prevent further damage, or when asked for help, these principals act quickly and decisively.

In the realm of instruction, principals' personal desires to intervene, even where they see opportunities for improvement, are tempered by their respect for teachers' knowledge and appreciation for their feelings. On instructional matters, therefore, they advise, suggest, provide information, and create opportunities for advanced training. Seldom do they issue directives. This softened entry into teachers' "territory" is accepted and quite effective in influencing changes in teacher behavior. With regard to the strategies we refer to collectively as gentle nudging, we offer the following recommendations for principals' consideration.

1. Know when to push and when to nudge.

   Effective principals do not hesitate to give specific direct instructions during crises. Also, when teachers request their help, they show genuine concern and take deliberate steps to help resolve the problem.

2. Know how to give advice, particularly regarding instruction.

   Rather than force teachers to comply with one preferred method, effective principals provide teachers with several acceptable alternatives. Further, they provide advice as offers of help from one colleague to another. The language of suggestion often takes the form of questions.

3. Provide training opportunities to reinforce goals and improve instruction.

   Effective principals assume that all teachers have room for professional growth. They share their own expertise with teachers, provide teachers opportunities to learn from one another, and invite external experts to assist in staff development.

4. Allow discretion in implementation of knowledge gained through staff development.

Perhaps one of the most essential requirements of successful training is the opportunity for teachers to evaluate the efficacy of changing their methods and respect for their ultimate judgments.

5. Assist teachers in evaluating newly attempted techniques.

New methods may be dropped by teachers because they initially require more time and effort. Efforts must be acknowledged and encouraged, and assistance should be provided in assessing the relative merit of the new approach.

6. Keep informed of new developments in curriculum and instruction and provide relevant information to teachers.

To have credibility as instructional leaders, principals must take the time to keep current on trends in curriculum and instruction. They can help teachers remain current and improve their skills if they sort, select, and disseminate professional materials of relevance to classroom and school performance. Materials should be limited to those that are relevant to a specific teacher's needs or to schoolwide goals. They should not be difficult to interpret and should provide meaningful, concrete suggestions for teacher use.

References

Allen, L., Glickman, C., & Hensley, F. (1998, April). *A search for accountability: The League of Professional Schools.* Paper presented at the annual meeting of the American Educational Research Association, San Diego, CA.

Blase, J., & Blase, J. (1994). *Empowering teachers: What successful principals do.* Thousand Oaks, CA: Corwin.

Blase, J., & Blase, J. (1997). *The fire is back: Principals sharing school governance.* Thousand Oaks, CA: Corwin.

Blase, J., & Blase, J. (1998). *Handbook of instructional leadership: How really good principals promote teaching and learning.* Thousand Oaks, CA: Corwin.

Blumberg, A. (1989). *School administration as a craft: Foundations of practice.* Boston: Allyn & Bacon.

Clift, R., Johnson, M., Holland, P., & Veal, M. L. (1992). Developing the potential for collaborative school leadership. *American Educational Research Journal, 29*(4), 877-908.

Hawley, W. D. (1988). Missing pieces of the educational reform agenda: Or, why the first and second waves may have missed the boat. *Educational Administration Quarterly, 24,* 416-437.

Kirby, P. C. (1992). Shared decision making: Moving from concerns about restrooms to concerns about classrooms. *Journal of School Leadership, 2,* 330-344.

Leithwood, K. (1994). Leadership for school restructuring. *Educational Administration Quarterly, 30*(4), 498-518.

Leithwood, K., & Jantzi, D. (1990). Transformational leadership: How principals can help reform school cultures. *School Effectiveness and School Improvement, 1,* 249-280.

Leithwood, K., Tomlinson, D., & Genge, M. (1996). Transformational school leadership. In K. Leithwood, J. Chapman, D. Corson, P. Hallinger, & A. Hart, *International handbook of educational leadership and administration* (pp. 785-840). Boston: Kluwer.

Maeroff, G. I. (1988). Blueprint for empowering teachers. *Phi Delta Kappan, 69,* 473-477.

Short, P. M., & Rinehart, J. S. (1992). School participant empowerment scale: Assessment of level of empowerment within the school environment. *Educational and Psychological Measurement, 52*(4), 951-960.

Weiss, C. (1990, April). *How much shared leadership is there in public high schools?* Paper presented at the annual meeting of the American Educational Research Association, Boston, MA.

Positive Use of Formal Authority 8

I have an authoritative principal, one who is warm but firm. Her excellent reputation and track record have proven that she makes wise decisions. Therefore, when she speaks, teachers listen and do. She transmits her requests to the faculty through meetings and newsletters. If the request is not carried out properly, she will reprimand that teacher privately. If it is carried out properly, she will sing your praises. She directly lets the faculty know at all times what she expects.

Nothing slips by my principal. She keeps me on my toes. Her goal is to provide a positive learning environment for the students. Nothing will stand in her way of accomplishing it. This has a positive effect on me. It makes me want to please her more by giving 110%.

—An elementary school teacher

*F*ormal authority is derived from the position held in a bureaucratic hierarchy. When asked to recollect influence strategies used by their principals, few teachers in our study volunteered that they comply out of respect for the principal's position alone. In fact, teachers and principals alike often view the exclusive reliance on formal authority by administrators as degrading and condescending. They resent being expected to suppress their intellect and creativity. According to Argyris (1957), workers are often expected to concede to formal authority because supervisors assume that workers, like infants, are incapable of self-direction and self-discipline. Given such assumptions, there is no need for collaborative planning; empowerment surely would lead to immature decisions. Accordingly, it is believed that workers prefer to be told what to do. Thus, the exercise of formal authority is necessary for organizational survival.

Dependence on formal authority alone flounders in the new era of restructured schools. Instead, choice and collaborative leadership are heralded by some as the only enduring means for reversing the failure of schooling in America (Glickman, 1993; Murphy & Louis, 1994). With teachers demanding a voice in school governance and public sentiment in favor of decentralization, any hint of autocracy raises the battle cry. Power is vested not in rank or title, but in those with valued expertise or strong interpersonal skills. Power and influence are functions of the person, not only the position.

Hersey, Blanchard, and Natemeyer (1976) developed a model describing seven bases of power. Bases of power determined by one's position include the power to dispense rewards, the power to sanction or punish, the power of the office (e.g., exercised through evaluation, hiring, and firing),[1] and the power based on knowing influential people. Three bases reside in the person: the power of expertise, the power of information, and the power of personality. Teacher satisfaction is negatively associated with overuse of position power. Clearly a positive relation exists between the use of personal power by administrators and higher levels of teacher professionalism. In part, the preference for personal power may be a function of sex-role stereotyping due to the large number of females in administrative positions in schools. Several research studies have confirmed that subordinates prefer that women leaders demonstrate strong consideration (e.g., kindness, thoughtfulness, respect) for followers. Although consideration also is viewed as an important leader behavior for males, it is frequently central to the leadership of female principals and has considerable influence with teachers (Beck, 1994; Noddings, 1992; Sergiovanni, 1992; Shakeshaft, 1987).

The type of organization—static or dynamic—may further influence preferences for a particular leadership style. In dynamic organizations, power is dispersed, individual initiative is valued, and decision making is shared. In such organizations, because there is a deemphasis on hierarchy and formal authority—realms in which males traditionally are perceived as more effective—women may be expected to emerge as leaders (Dunlap & Schmuck, 1995; Noddings, 1992; Women's Educational Equity Act Publishing Center, 1990). Problems associated with position power in education, then, may be a function of both the increasing professionalization of teaching, which transforms schools into more dynamic organizations, and sex-role stereotyping, which limits the options available to female principals for successfully influencing teachers.

Effective Use of Formal Authority

Although the research on sex-role expectations is limited and inconclusive, there is considerable evidence that people prefer a democratic style of leadership from leaders of either sex. According to Hersey et al. (1976), more mature (i.e., experienced, willing, competent) followers are less influenced by the use of position power. The effect of formal authority, therefore, is attenuated by the restructuring of schools where teachers are viewed as professionals (i.e., mature subordinates) and where shared decision making is valued.

Given this devaluing of formal authority, it is not surprising that the teachers in our study qualified their responses to its influence. They reported that open and effective principals do use the authority of their office to influence teacher behavior, but teachers noted in all cases that principals do so equitably and respectfully. In several cases, teachers rationalized that principals need to rely on the power of their position to influence less competent teachers. This is consistent with Hersey et al.'s (1976) situational leadership theory—less mature followers (in this case, less competent teachers) respond more readily to use of position power.

Our teachers also reported that principals use authority to uphold district polices and reinforce fundamental norms such as fairness and maximum use of allocated learning time. Frequently reported instructional goals are related to student rights and needs:

> She has always insisted that what is done for one class must be done for all 10 classes. It was very hard for me to begin to think of not just my class of first graders and what they need and what I can do for them. After five years, I have seen the results of caring that every child in the first grade learn to read and not just my class of 25. It has made me more aware of all children in my grade level and has helped me help new teachers so that their classes could achieve as well as mine.

Effective principals demand that all students have equal exposure to content and that they be tested fairly. They told the teachers in our study to ensure "bell-to-bell teaching" and early involvement from parents. Punctuality, compliance with state standards and district policies, and awareness of duties and responsibilities are among the noninstructional goals associated with the use of authority. Only in rare cases is authority used explicitly to demonstrate power or "show who's the boss."

Accepted Uses of Authority

According to teachers, principals exercise authority when they assign specific duties to teachers or appoint teachers to committees. They use authority when they announce a new instructional objective or school policy. They use authority when they enforce rules, require participation, or mandate action. In contrast to most other strategies reported by teachers, authority is viewed as quite direct. As the terms associated with its use imply, it is exercised unilaterally; when used, little negotiation or bargaining is evident.

How then are some principals able to use authority effectively without appearing to be forceful or insensitive? Apparently, the use of authority is accepted because teachers believe it is used fairly to achieve positive outcomes for others—not as a manipulative tactic for the principal's personal gain. The following excerpts from teachers' responses demonstrate this nonmanipulative, humanitarian use of authority:

- ◆ "He requires teachers to communicate in a positive manner with students."
- ◆ "He assigns work to everyone equally."
- ◆ "My principal does not want us to allow students to fail because they refuse to turn in work. We must talk to them, contact parents, and send students to the office if they do not do their work. Only after we have exhausted all methods can we give them a zero."
- ◆ "He required that we write a positive letter for each 6-week grading period to parents for a student that we felt deserved recognition."

At times, principals use authority to make final decisions after soliciting input from teachers: "He explains what needs to be done, answers questions that anyone might have, evaluates suggestions, and selects a course of action." This limited "consultative" approach is accepted by some teachers because decisions are perceived to be based on school need and an awareness of teachers' problems. As one teacher commented, her principal made most decisions, but only after "listening to the flow of the school." Often teachers accept their principals' authority because of the principal's history of making competent and consistent decisions:

> [My principal] is firm but fair with the way that she deals with faculty and students. When teachers don't follow the rules, she calls them into her office and informs them that they will follow the rules or she will find someone who can. I feel secure in the knowledge that the rules are in place for everyone without regard to area taught, [whether one is a] coach or noncoach, etc.

The exercise of authority has mixed effects on the feelings and behaviors of teachers in our study. Approximately 60% of the feelings associated with authority are positive. Teachers used "comfortable," "secure," and "encouraged" to describe their reactions to this form of influence. Several teachers reported initially having negative reactions to the use of authority, but their feelings changed when they understood the principals' rationale for its use. For example, one teacher was upset that teachers had not been involved in preplanning, but she accepted the principal's plan because it was educationally sound. She rationalized that "if just one student learns, it will be worth it."

Behaviorally, most teachers comply with the wishes of principals who use authority. Specific effects include more positive attitudes toward students, increased contact with parents, and adherence to rules and deadlines. Not surprisingly, Leithwood and his colleagues (1998) found that use of contingent rewards—the ability to dispense rewards based on position of authority—is often related to transformational leadership behaviors that have positive effects on teachers and students.

Negative Effect

In the introduction to this chapter, we discuss the problems related to the use of formal authority. It should not be inferred from our data that these obstacles are entirely overcome by open and effective principals simply because they recognize appropriate uses of authority. Quite the contrary: Of the teachers who reported authority as one means of influence used by their principals, 40% identified negative outcomes connected with its use. They noted feelings of anger, resentment, guilt, rebelliousness, depression, intimidation, and manipulation.

The remarks of some teachers reveal that they equate the use of authority with their principals' assumptions that teachers are immature—incapable of setting their own priorities, managing time, or assuming responsibility. Very often, teachers explained, these principals implement and enforce rules to monitor teacher behavior.

Sign-in sheets were mentioned by several teachers as an ongoing source of frustration. One teacher noted how monitoring of punctuality could be used to induce feelings of guilt and humiliation: "[The principal] takes up the sign-in sheet when people come in late. This makes you be on time or you must go see her to sign in."

Planning is another area of teachers' lives monitored by principals. Teachers often are required to turn in weekly lesson plans. Although the practice may be district mandated, some teachers

view its strict implementation as an unnecessary display of authority by the principal:

> I resent the use of time to write specific lesson plans that I
> feel could be used in a more productive way. I do it because
> I have to, just like I did in college. But at times I get angry
> because I need that time to have parent conferences, work
> on student lessons, meet with individual students to discuss
> goals.

Finally, principals monitor teachers' grading practices. Some
require that teachers submit copies of their grading policies each
year. Others reserve the right to preview report card grades before
the cards are sent home to parents. The most resented practice,
however, is an order from the principal to change a student's grade.
Some teachers eventually compromise their standards to avoid
confrontation: "I am more hesitant in sending home failing grades
and unsatisfactory conduct grades." When confronted, others
buckle to authority by principals: "We do what we are assigned . . .
You get in trouble if you buck the system"; "When you don't, you
get reprimanded as a child would." Although teachers comply with
their principals' directives, principals' self-appointed veto power
over student grades has bitter repercussions:

> I am angry and frustrated. I was disappointed in myself for
> not refusing to change the grade the child earned . . . It's
> unfair to give a false picture of a child's academic success. I
> do not feel that it was ethical for an administrator to dis-
> regard the evaluation of a child.

The Selective Use of Authority

The reader may now be left with a mixed message with regard to
the use of authority. Although it is frequently reported as an effective
influence strategy, its use often leaves teachers feeling resentful.
Teachers seem to accept that there are some appropriate times to
draw on legitimate power, but they seldom feel that the time is

appropriate for them. Thus, authority must be invoked with extreme care. It should not be used to perpetuate humiliating rules, nor should it be used without justification. With these caveats in mind, we offer the following suggestions for the selective use of authority.

1. Work to change bureaucratic rules and policies that reduce teachers' status.

We do not advocate anarchy, but we do recognize that principals create rules for control of the few who are not self-managing. A professional (adult) view of teachers requires that conditions that cast them as children be eliminated. Peters (1987) advises managers to eliminate bureaucratic rules and humiliating conditions. Sign-in sheets, detailed lesson plans, and close scrutiny of teacher-assigned grades are three practices that teachers find demeaning. Consider eliminating them. If such rules are mandated by the school district, work to get them changed. When policies are violated, monitor only the violator.

2. Where authority is necessary to enforce necessary rules or policies, justify its use in ethical terms.

Keep in mind that effective and open principals used authority to influence teachers in our study, and that 60% of the teachers reported no negative feelings associated with this strategy. Many rationalized its use because it was equitable to teachers and in the best interest of students. Student grades, for example, should be objectively defensible. Principals may wish to review teachers' grading practices or assigned grades to guarantee fair treatment of students. They may insist that teachers exercise all available means of assistance before failing students. These uses of authority will be tolerated more easily by teachers if the humanitarian treatment of students is always the stated purpose.

3. Solicit input in creating policies that may have to be enforced through the exercise of authority.

Teachers are less resentful over the use of authority to enforce decisions that are made collectively. Granting teachers a voice in school decisions serves two purposes here: It is based on a professional view of teachers that buffers the negative effect of formal authority, and it creates ownership for the decision. Thus, if monitoring or enforcement through authority becomes necessary, teachers are likely to be more supportive. To resolve the lesson plan dilemma, for example, teachers might be asked to create a method for ensuring that all teachers are prepared for their classes, but one that is more than a perfunctory exercise in documentation. They may develop a plan for verbal checks, simplified written plans, or peer monitoring. If given the freedom to develop their own policies, teachers are likely to become self-policing.

4. Accept that there are appropriate times to exercise authority.

Research on sex-role stereotyping suggests that subordinates may expect less authoritative behavior from females, but this research is far from conclusive. Principals might look to situational leadership theories for guidance rather than comply with role expectations. Situational theorists suggest that the use of authority should be determined by the maturity of teachers; that is, their willingness and ability to perform as expected in relation to the demands of a given task. Teachers who are less competent or less experienced require more directive guidance ✳ and closer monitoring. As an example, teachers whose daily lesson plans have been impeccable for the first three months of the school year might be allowed to turn in monthly summary plans for the remainder of the year. Of course, any practice that may be construed as unequal treatment of teachers must be objective, and the basis for differential treatment (e.g., records of poor lesson plans or number of times teacher arrived late) must be documented.

Note

1. It is interesting to note that French and Raven (1968), and later Hersey, Blanchard, and Natemeyer (1976), refer to the power of office as *legitimate* power. They use the term in a legalistic sense.

If *legitimate* is used to mean valid or acceptable, then the most legitimate power from a teacher's perspective is personal power.

References

Argyris, C. (1957). *Personality and organization.* New York: Harper & Row.

Beck, L. G. (1994). *Reclaiming educational administration as a caring profession.* New York: Teachers College Press.

Dunlap, D. M., & Schmuck, P. A. (1995). *Women leading in education.* Albany: State University of New York Press.

French, J. R. P., & Raven, B. H. (1968). Bases of social power. In D. Cartwright & A. Zander (Eds.), *Group dynamics: Research and theory* (pp. 259-270). New York: Harper & Row.

Glickman, C. D. (1993). *Renewing America's schools: A guide for school-based action.* San Francisco: Jossey-Bass.

Hersey, P., Blanchard, K., & Natemeyer, W. E. (1976). Situational leadership, perception, and the impact of power. *Group and Organization Studies, 4,* 418-428.

Leithwood, K., Tomlinson, D., & Genge, M. (1998). Transformational school leadership. In K. Leithwood, J. Chapman, D. Corson, P. Hallinger, & A. Hart (Eds.), *International handbook of educational leadership and administration* (pp. 785-840). Boston: Kluwer.

Murphy, J., & Louis, K. S. (1994). *Reshaping the principalship: Insights from transformational reform efforts.* Thousand Oaks, CA: Corwin.

Noddings, N. (1992). *The challenge to care in schools.* New York: Teachers College Press.

Peters, T. (1987). *Thriving on chaos: Handbook for a management revolution.* New York: Harper & Row.

Sergiovanni, T. J. (1992). *Moral leadership: Getting to the heart of school improvement.* San Francisco: Jossey-Bass.

Shakeshaft, C. (1987). *Women in educational administration.* Newbury Park, CA: Sage.

Women's Educational Equity Act Publishing Center. (1990). *Women in school administration.* Newton, MA: Author.

Mirrors to the Possible

Our principal is supportive and personally concerned with his teachers' professional careers and outside interests. He is involved with students' extracurricular activities such as Special Olympics. He takes an interest in classroom activities and takes time to visit classrooms informally. He brags to visitors about his teachers and their programs. He has a positive attitude about his job, which encourages a good attitude [among others]. He is very concerned with keeping an upbeat attitude in a school situation that tends to be depressing and discouraging. It works. Teachers in the school are as concerned and involved with the principal as he is with us.

—*An elementary school teacher*

o this point, we have discussed strategies of effective school principals that teachers in our study recognize as particularly powerful in influencing their behavior. But the teachers also commented extensively on the personality of leaders. They identified certain aspects of their principals' personality and demeanor that contributed to principals' effectiveness as leaders. In particular, the teachers found that effective principals are highly visible and model attitudes and behaviors consistent with personal values and with the expectations they hold for teachers. Teachers see these principals as expressing changes in schooling that are both desirable and possible.

Personality has long been recognized as an important dimension of leader effectiveness. Some people are more inspiring, more likable, more appealing than others. These persons frequently emerge as leaders. *Referent power* is the term used to refer to one's ability to influence based on personality. In the extreme form, it is called charisma.

Max Weber borrowed the concept of charisma from theology, where it was considered to be a gift bestowed by God. For Weber, charisma is a mystical, magnetic attraction that some individuals acquire in times of crisis. Others follow the charismatic, believing that they too will be connected to transcendent powers by virtue of association with the charismatic (Bass, 1988).

The definition of charisma has evolved since Weber's conceptualization. Many theorists no longer believe that charismatic leadership emerges only in situations of crisis, for example. But the exact qualifications of the charismatic are no less clear today than they were when charisma was believed to be a gift from God. According to Bass (1988), two essential elements of the charismatic relationship are a strong desire by followers to identify with the leader, and the leader's possession of certain abilities, traits, and interests. Among the latter, Bass includes emotional expressiveness or dramatic flair, self-confidence, conviction in one's beliefs, eloquence, insight, and high levels of energy.

Are the effective principals described in our study charismatic? According to teachers, aspects of principals' personality that are most influential are their honesty, optimism, and consideration. Further, principals are able to (and do) model the behavior they expect from teachers, and they are highly visible in their schools. Although the principals described to us are certainly liked and respected by their teachers, they are not simply depicted as dramatic, highly inspirational, and magnetic; that is, few are described in terms typically associated with charisma.

Lawler (1984) argues that more educated followers are less influenced by charisma than the less educated. Thus, in organizations of workers with higher levels of skill and training, dramatic appeal is a less powerful form of persuasion than expertise and consideration. Furthermore, there may be less magic and more logic to the personality of leaders than formerly acknowledged. Kouzes and Posner (1990) studied the personal traits and characteristics most admired in leaders. In study after study, they found that the overwhelming choice of managers and executives—the most essential test of one's ability to influence—is honesty. Inspiration ranks fourth, after honesty, competence, and being forward looking.

The responses of teachers in our study are consistent with Kouzes and Posner's (1990) findings. Effective principals are repeatedly described as honest. They demonstrate their competence by modeling the skills and behaviors they expect from teachers, and they maintain very positive attitudes and sincere beliefs that they will improve education for students. Teachers also added consideration as an important personal attribute.

Leadership based on the values of honesty, optimism, and consideration differs in fundamental ways from leadership based on charisma. Most notable among the differences is that the former is grounded in morality, whereas the latter is grounded in personality. Moral leaders incorporate an ethic of caring into a vision of what is best and possible for all students (Beck & Murphy, 1994; Bolman & Deal, 1995; Marshall, Patterson, Rogers, & Steele, 1996; Noddings, 1992). In achieving their vision, they ask no more of others than they expect from themselves. Their actions and words are consistent, and they are genuine in their interactions with others.

Numerous scholars have raised questions about the field of educational administration's preoccupation with bureaucracy and failure to recognize the place of values in discourse (Beck & Murphy, 1994; Blase & Anderson, 1995; Evers & Lakomski, 1993; Hodgkinson, 1991; Willower, 1994). William Foster (1991, p. 20) criticizes the field of educational administration for its "bureaucratic concern with efficiency" and banning of values from discourse. In the scientific-positivist tradition that has dominated educational administration, he argues, decisions are evaluated on the basis of rules and procedures, rather than on the basis of what is moral or right. Education can no more be amoral than can it be apolitical, however. Foster argues that administrators could help transform schooling through open critique, caring, and inclusion. Administrators who are able to make things happen in schools do so "not because of their scientific training and their judicious use of principles of management, but because of their personal and moral presence, their sense of 'what's right,' and their attention to people's needs" (p. 7).

It appears, then, that principals in our study may have been effective largely because they were viewed as moral leaders by teachers. The first standard in the American Association of School

Administrators' (1976) code of ethics states, "A school administrator makes the well-being of students the fundamental value of all decision making and actions." A key theme in the data generated by our study is that goals associated with principals' influence strategies truly focus on "what's best for children." It may be that whatever the strategies used, principals' behaviors are ultimately judged against teachers' own moral codes.

The Personality of Leaders

Effective school leaders are frequently described as optimistic, honest, and considerate. Behaviors such as modeling and visibility convey these values.

Optimism

The positive attitude of principals was noted by several teachers in our study. These principals are perceived as enjoying their jobs and believing in the abilities of their staffs. They also are described as problem solvers who had particularly good relationships with their faculties and students. Teachers reported increases in self-esteem, security, and motivation resulting from principals' optimism. Some indicated that their attitudes also became more positive:

> She has a very positive feeling about our school. She enjoys her job and it is reflected to the rest of the teachers . . . She faces every day as a new day with new challenges. I try to do the same. I don't mind coming to school this year. When the alarm goes off, I'm "up and at them" this year.

Extra effort was reported by other teachers: "The strategy makes me give 100% effort to the school and my class." Another summarized the benefits of a positive approach: "It makes me feel good about what I do."

Martin Seligman (1991), a noted psychologist, is careful to define optimism as the power of nonnegative thinking, not as unjustifiable positivity. The optimist avoids catastrophizing; in times of

adversity, consequences are not distorted and are seen as insur-
mountable. Thus, the school principal who sees education as being
in a state of crisis is neither positive nor negative. The optimist will
explain the causes of the crisis in terms that are external, specific,
and temporary. The pessimist will explain the crisis as internal
("I should have done more"), pervasive (e.g., "teachers are less
competent than they used to be"), and permanent. By monitoring
our explanations of the events in our lives, Seligman claims, we can
learn to be more optimistic.

Seligman presents forceful research evidence to suggest that
optimists are happier and healthier and live longer than pessimists.
More relevant to the present discussion, optimists tend to be liked
more and are more successful in their work. Through analysis of
campaign speeches, for example, Seligman and his colleagues found
that successful U.S. presidential candidates tend to be more optimistic than their opponents. Our findings confirm that optimism may
indeed be a significant factor in leader effectiveness.

Honesty

As used by teachers in our study, honesty refers to the principal's truthfulness, as well as openness and consistency between
words and actions. One teacher explained: "There is no phony
baloney . . . She [the principal] will not tell you one thing and do
another." Honesty was noted in principals' ability to communicate
straightforwardly both positive and negative feedback to teachers.
Honest principals confront teachers' weaknesses and acknowledge
their strengths:

> Our principal is totally honest in his dealings with the
> faculty. He is direct with what he feels are our strengths and
> weaknesses and is always willing to help solve any problem
> that might arise . . . [This] keeps me open-minded in my
> dealings with my students . . . and others on the faculty.

Also, nonmanipulation of teachers is viewed as a dimension of
honesty that fosters collaboration: "I feel that the principal is working with me and I with him, not for him." Teacher satisfaction and

effort also are associated with honesty: "You enjoy working for people of this nature, thus you want to improve."

Consideration

Consideration has been recognized as a major dimension of leader behavior in most theories of organizational effectiveness. Alternately termed *people orientation* or *concern for people*, consideration is reported to be related to employee satisfaction by most major leadership theorists (see, e.g., Bass, 1990; Blake & Mouton, 1964; Fiedler, 1967; Hersey & Blanchard, 1977; Stogdill, 1963). In a major study of school effectiveness, Uline, Miller, and Tschannen-Moran (1998) measured two aspects of school effectiveness: instrumental and expressive functions. Expressive functions affect a school's social cohesion and build school culture. Activities associated with trust, teacher and student commitment, and morale are considered expressive activities. These researchers found that both expressive and instrumental activities are significantly correlated with overall school effectiveness and student achievement.

Our teachers defined consideration as exhibiting a sincere interest in "teachers as human beings." A considerate principal was described as one who "shows a genuine concern for how I am doing . . . [one who] makes a point to say hello." Considerate principals were viewed as nondiscriminating; they show concern for all teachers. They express interest in their teachers' lives during both happy and sad events. One high school teacher gave an example:

> My principal was very understanding and flexible the times that I had to be absent due to hospitalization of family members. His cooperation and attempts to make my return to school smoother were above and beyond the call of duty. I feel that I've been treated with kindness and respect. I, in turn, tend to have a more compassionate attitude toward my students and their individual situations.

Effects associated with consideration include enhanced self-esteem ("If he believes in me then I can believe in myself") and improved performance ("I come early and stay late and do maximum work because I know my work is appreciated"). Considerate principals serve as models for teachers. Several teachers reported becoming more considerate and empathic in their dealings with children and fellow teachers. Thus, principals serve as mirrors of appropriate human interaction:

♦ "Teachers act more as friends, helpers, and resource persons. Students know we care about them and provide encouragement for them to meet their daily challenges."

♦ "[The principal's consideration] helps to promote warmth in our faculty. We cooperate with each other and express concern for each other."

♦ "Because our principal shows caring and concern, I feel the need to reciprocate; I want to give him back what he gives us."

Personality Manifested: Mirroring the Possible

The optimism, honesty, and consideration of effective principals are revealed in their daily interactions with students and teachers. These traits reflect the principals' values. As such, effective teachers also are expected to be optimistic, honest, and considerate. The principals described in our study offer countless opportunities for teachers to acquire similar values by revealing themselves as mirrors to the possible. Effective principals are highly visible and serve as models of appropriate attitudes and behaviors.

Modeling

In earlier chapters, we discuss how effective principals encourage participation by participating as equal members in groups of teachers. As promoters of teacher development, they themselves are avid readers of professional literature, seeking new means of improvement. Expecting teachers to use positive disciplinary approaches with students, they provide examples of such techniques. At times, they also demonstrate teaching techniques. Thus, modeling is used quite effectively to reinforce other strategies of influence.

Modeling as a general influence strategy was recognized by several teachers in the study. Modeling also is a key factor of transformational leadership in numerous studies of principals' effectiveness (Leithwood, Tomlinson, & Genge, 1996). Principals enact their expectations for teacher performance through their own behavior. As one teacher explained, "My principal seems to administer by behavior [rather than by] policy. For example, he asks that we dress professionally, monitor the halls between classes, attend extracurricular activities, and contribute to the United Way. He does all of these." Another explained:

> [My principal] is a very positive person. She conveys her feelings about school and the kids to us without being overbearing or obnoxious. She does not ask us to do anything she has not already done herself or would not do. She does not complain about things that she cannot change. She makes the best of all situations. She is a good role model. When I get angry about something, I think about how she would handle the situation.

Expected behaviors modeled by the principals include appropriate dress, punctuality, effective teaching, positive discipline, praise for students, and extra effort. Without exception, teachers reported that modeling influences them to behave in ways consistent with the principal's implicit expectations. With regard to extra effort, for example, a teacher commented that "many of [the principal's] requests might be viewed as beyond the call of duty, but, because of the principal's modeling, they seem to be part of the job." Another remarked that she tried approaches to student behavior in the hallways that she had seen her principal use effectively. Overall, teachers reported that modeling is a highly effective strategy of influence that leaves them feeling "comfortable," "proud," "aware" (of alternative techniques), and "positive."

Visibility

As a principal's visibility increases, so too do his or her opportunities to model effective behavior. According to our teachers, some principals clearly are more comfortable in hallways and classrooms than in their offices.

Sheppard (1996) synthesizes the research on instructional leadership behaviors, especially those linked to student achievement outcomes. Sheppard confirms a strong positive relationship between leadership behaviors exhibited by principals, such as maintaining high visibility, and teacher commitment, professional involvement, and innovativeness. Similarly, from a study of teachers throughout the United States, Blase and Blase (1998) found that principal visibility led to significant increases in teacher motivation, self-esteem, sense of security, morale, and, to a lesser degree, teacher reflection.

Andrews and Soder (1987) relate gains in mathematics and reading scores of low-achieving students to four instructional leadership roles: instructional resource, resource provider, communicator, and visible presence. In later work, visibility was found to be particularly influential when new programs or techniques are being implemented (Bamburg & Andrews, 1989). As Kouzes and Posner (1990) observe, "[leaders] demonstrate what is important by how they spend their time, by the priorities on their agenda, by the questions they ask, by the people they see, the places they go, and the behaviors and results that they recognize and reward" (p. 200).

Teachers reported that effective principals are visible, both in the hallways and in classrooms. Different goals are attributed to visibility in each setting. Visibility in the hallways is deemed to be an effective manner of communicating support to both teachers and students. Implicit in the principal's presence is an expectation for appropriate student behavior between classes and an offer of assistance to teachers in matters of discipline should they so desire. Visibility in the classroom is associated more typically with expectations for instruction. Expectations for the use of allocated instructional time are implied by the principal's presence, as are expectations regarding implementation of specific instructional strategies. One elementary teacher described her principal's influence through visibility:

> The principal is extremely involved with all grades and their curricula. She visits the classrooms regularly (two times per week) to make sure that all teachers are on task. She walks around to see if the children are involved and

participating in that particular subject. If not, she would place her hands on their shoulders to get their attention and make sure that they are then attentive. This type of discipline is very effective for all children.

The teachers experienced visibility as positive and nonthreatening. They indicated that visibility in the hallways helps to preempt some discipline problems: "It helps him to see problems before they snowball into serious ones." The principal's presence also affords the opportunity to model optimism: "My principal frequently roams the halls during breaks between classes. He is very friendly and supportive. His positive attitude overflows both to students and to faculty."

Classroom visibility is sporadic for some of the principals and routine for others; some inform teachers of classroom visits, whereas others drop in unannounced. The length of classroom visits also varies widely, as reported in our study, from a few minutes to a whole class period. Some principals walk around the class to "see what the students are busy doing." Others become more fully involved with the class activity: "She visits my class while we are doing laboratory activities . . . participates with the students . . . asks them questions . . . asks me questions. She demonstrates to the students that learning is a lifelong activity."

Teachers indicated that principals usually provide some form of feedback to teachers after visiting their classrooms. Consistent with the strategy of suggestion discussed in Chapter 7, feedback is presented as advisory. The teachers view visibility as an effective and acceptable strategy because it is accompanied by genuine interest and support. It is not viewed as obtrusive or punitive. Instead, the teachers associate visibility with opportunities for improvement ("You can correct weak points with her help") and increased accountability ("Even though I am a conscientious teacher, I need monitors. Unscheduled pop-in visits are motivational.").

The motivational effect of principals' visibility in the classroom is quite powerful. Numerous examples suggest that although anxiety levels are heightened somewhat by the principal's visit, teachers work harder, are more innovative, and feel better about their own performance as a result:

♦ "As much as [visits] scare me, I like them because they bring me back to task."

♦ "Not knowing when I might be visited, I stay on task more often than I might if these visits didn't occur."

♦ "I try things I previously frowned on—outside labs, field trips."

♦ "[The principal's visits] caused me to think more about my class and my role as a teacher. I am aware that I am accountable for performance."

Mirrors Seldom Lie

We have presented three personality traits—honesty, consideration, and optimism—that appear to be common to effective and open principals. These traits are evident in principals' frequent inter-actions with their staffs (i.e., in their visibility) and in the consistency between their expectations and their own actions (i.e., modeling). If modeling and visibility are particularly effective in producing desirable outcomes in teachers for honest, caring, and positive prin-cipals, the implications for schools led by manipulative, inconsid-erate, and negative principals are terrifying. Principals in the middle—those whose values are less explicit, who are sometimes thoughtful and positive, sometimes distant and gloomy—also emit constant messages to teachers. Teachers learn to be guarded and protective, afraid to trust the unpredictable. The implications for principals are weighty indeed.

Leaders may serve as mirrors to what is possible and what is right for the individuals they serve. But mirrors also can reflect barriers to human potential—lack of trust, feeling, and hope. As all of us who have stopped counting birthdays will attest, mirrors seldom lie. What is reflected to the observer is what the observer has become. If principals are reliable mirrors of what schools will be-come, we must develop moral leaders. Our data suggest that moral leaders abide by these principles.

1. Do not become so concerned with becoming effective as to ignore the affective.

Consideration of others—an ethic of caring—is fundamental to moral leadership. Although this aspect of leadership can be improved through careful attention to others, the implications for leader selection should be obvious. Attention to moral fortitude should precede all other qualifications, including demonstrated mastery of certain managerial and instructional skills, in the selection of school leaders.

2. Practice being more optimistic.

According to Seligman (1991), a more positive attitude can be acquired by monitoring our explanations of life's successes and failures. Specifically, we must learn to recognize that adversity is usually temporary, specific, and externally created. Although learning to become more optimistic is a difficult task, its advantages are clearly documented.

3. Be visible, but beware the power of the mirror.

Effective leaders know that their behavior is regarded as the standard of performance. They therefore avail themselves of all opportunities to model the behaviors they expect in others. To become mirrors to what is right and possible, they must ensure that their behavior is above reproach. They must be honest in their interactions with others; the values they convey must be consistent in words and actions as well as over time. As long as principals are in contact with teachers, they are transmitting their values and expectations. The burden of the mirror is that it never stops reflecting.

References

American Association of School Administrators. (1976). *AASA statement of ethics for school administrators and procedural guidelines.* Arlington, VA: Author.

Andrews, R. L., & Soder, R. (1987). Principal instructional leadership and school achievement. *Instructional Leadership, 44,* 9-11.

Bamburg, J. D., & Andrews, R. L. (1989, March). *Putting effective schools research to work: The process of change and the role of the principal.* Paper presented at the annual meeting of the American Educational Research Association, San Francisco, CA.

Bass, B. M. (1988). Evolving perspectives on charismatic leadership. In J. A. Conger & R. N. Kanungo (Eds.), *Charismatic leadership: Behind the mystique of exceptional leadership* (pp. 40-77). San Francisco: Jossey-Bass.

Bass, B. M. (1990). *Bass and Stogdill's handbook of leadership: Theory, research, and managerial applications* (3rd ed.). New York: Free Press.

Beck, L. G., & Murphy, J. (1994). *Ethics in educational leadership programs: An expanding role.* Thousand Oaks, CA: Corwin.

Blake, R., & Mouton, J. (1964). *The managerial grid.* Houston, TX: Gulf.

Blase, J., & Anderson, G. (1995). *The micropolitics of educational leadership: From control to empowerment.* London: Caswell.

Blase, J., & Blase, J. (1998). *Handbook of instructional leadership: How really good principals promote teaching and learning.* Thousand Oaks, CA: Corwin.

Bolman, L. G., & Deal, T. E. (1995). *Leading with soul.* San Francisco: Jossey-Bass.

Evers, C. W., & Lakomski, G. (1993). Cognition, values, and organizational structure: Hodgkinson in perspective. *Journal of Educational Administration and Foundations, 8*(1), 45-57.

Fiedler, F. (1967). *A theory of leadership effectiveness.* New York: McGraw-Hill.

Foster, W. (1991, April). *Moral theory, transformation, and leadership in school settings.* Paper presented at the annual meeting of the American Educational Research Association, Chicago, IL.

Hersey, P., & Blanchard, K. (1977). *Management of organizational behavior: Utilizing human resources.* Englewood Cliffs, NJ: Prentice Hall.

Hodgkinson, C. (1991). *Educational leadership: The moral art.* Albany: State University of New York Press.

Kouzes, J. M., & Posner, B. Z. (1990). *The leadership challenge: How to get extraordinary things done in organizations.* San Francisco: Jossey-Bass.

Lawler, E. E., III. (1984). Leadership in participative organizations. In J. G. Hunt, D. Hosking, C. A. Schreisheim, & R. Stewart (Eds.), *Leaders and managers: International perspectives on managerial behavior and leadership*. Elmsford, NY: Pergamon.

Leithwood, K., Tomlinson, D., & Genge, M. (1996). Transformational school leadership. In K. Leithwood, J. Chapman, D. Corson, P. Hallinger, & A. Hart (Eds.), *International handbook of educational leadership and administration* (pp. 785-840). Boston: Kluwer.

Marshall, C., Patterson, J. A., Rogers, D. L., & Steele, J. R. (1996). Caring as career: An alternative perspective for educational administration. *Educational Administration Quarterly, 32*(2), 271-294.

Noddings, N. (1992). *The challenge to care in schools.*. New York: Teachers College Press.

Seligman, M. E. P. (1991). *Learned optimism*. New York: Knopf.

Sheppard, B. (1996). Exploring the transformational nature of instructional leadership. *Alberta Journal of Educational Research, 42*(4), 325-344.

Stogdill, R. (1963). *Manual for the LBDQ-Form 12: An experimental revision*. Columbus: Ohio State University, Bureau of Business Research.

Uline, C. L., Miller, D. M., & Tschannen-Moran, M. (1998). School effectiveness: The underlying dimensions. *Educational Administration Quarterly, 34*(4), 462-483.

Willower, D. (1994). *Educational administration: Inquiry, values, practice*. Lancaster, PA: Technomic.

Conclusions, Caveats, and Challenges

To change our guidance program, the principal involved the faculty in devising a plan. The major input came from the creative and technical talents of the staff. We brainstormed what was wrong with the current situation and described what we wanted. Staff members researched program options and visited schools using the preferred programs. . . . At times in the process I wondered why [the principal] didn't just decide. [Collaborative problem solving] can feel like more work to teachers. But the staff got very excited and very supportive. That was not the case at other schools. By empowering and validating teachers, change occurs, schools become more positive and more effective.

—An elementary school teacher

*I*n preceding chapters, we describe a number of strategies and related practices that teachers in our study associate with the effectiveness of their principals. We attempted to use the teachers' words as much as possible to portray leader behaviors as teachers themselves view such behaviors. Specific practices reported by teachers are used to elaborate on the use of each strategy. For example, practices associated with the strategy of involvement include an open-door policy, solicitation of suggestions, delegation, and formal team structures. Administrative support ("leading by standing behind") includes providing basic materials, reducing interference to instructional time, paying tuition for professional conferences, and assisting teachers in matters of student discipline.

In all cases, we describe the strategies and tactics that emerged from our data; that is, descriptions of effective principals are accounts of what enhances teaching from the teachers' perspectives. Who better to tell us how to influence teacher performance positively?

Based on teachers' reports, we conclude that principals who are open and effective:

♦ Praise teachers' efforts

♦ Convey high expectations for teacher and student performance

♦ Actively involve teachers in decision making

♦ Provide teachers the autonomy (freedom) to try creative approaches

♦ Support teachers by providing materials, training opportunities, and backing in student discipline matters

♦ Nudge teachers to consider alternative solutions to instruction and discipline problems

♦ Judiciously evoke the power of authority

♦ Consistently model effective practice

Our data indicate that individual principals use most of the strategies we describe and often simultaneously. Further, principals are honest, optimistic, considerate, and highly visible in their schools. They seem to enjoy their work and infect others with a positive outlook.

Teachers reported that these strategies have many positive effects on their thinking, attitudes, and behavior. Most frequently mentioned are enhanced self-esteem and confidence, greater sensitivity to student needs, job satisfaction, commitment and loyalty, flexibility and creativity, extra time and effort, and improved faculty morale.

On the basis of teacher reports, we present suggestions for principals with regard to each successful influence strategy. These are offered only as suggestions and not as prescriptions for effective leader behavior. The reader must cautiously and reflectively consider the applicability of each suggestion in the context of particular school settings. In fact, a small amount of negative data did surface regarding open and effective principals. In describing strategies used by principals to influence their behavior, a few teachers reported that their effective principals occasionally use coercion or authoritarianism to gain their compliance. It should also be stressed that teachers rated these strategies as very ineffective. When used, they provoked resistance or alienation in teachers.

On Knowing How and Knowing When

Our findings are generally consistent with other research on effective principals (e.g., Barth, 1990; Leithwood, Tomlinson, & Genge, 1996; Sergiovanni, 1992). Still, there is much debate about what constitutes effective practice in educational administration. Indeed, Wimpelberg, Teddlie, and Stringfield (1989) argue that what little we know about effective schools has not been examined through different contextual lenses. Context-specific characteristics about schooling would likely determine the appropriate leadership practices in particular settings.

Because problems and contexts are idiosyncratic, it is not possible to tell principals specifically what to do to promote successful teaching. How does the practitioner know when to use particular strategies?

Donald Schön (1983, 1991) describes a new breed of professional whom he calls the "reflective practitioner." He argues that some professions, particularly in the social sciences, do not conform to preexisting understandings of professional practice. Rules and procedures cannot be specified a priori for all problems of practice. Instead, problems are unique; their resolution must be determined "on the spot." The practitioner must almost simultaneously frame the problem, determine alternative courses of action, choose from among the alternatives, apply and test one solution, and then reframe and retest based on the results. Schön calls this process "reflection in action."

In organizations as complex and dynamic as schools, events unfold rapidly and new problems continually arise. Problem solving must consist of what Schön (1983) calls a "reflective conversation with the situation" (p. 242), a mental testing of assumptions while activating solutions. In contrast to pure science, no definitive theories or facts capture the reality of schools and allow us to resolve problems easily. Instead, the practitioner must draw on knowledge gained from the theory and research of the profession as well as knowledge acquired through experience. In addition to what they have learned from training and research, principals do have the benefit of experience in specific contexts.

Like Schön, we wish to acknowledge the crucial role that experience and reflection play—indeed must play—in determining how best to lead a school. The reflective practitioner uses both experience and science reflectively in framing and solving unique problems in varying contexts.

Of course, many of the behaviors or characteristics that we describe throughout this book would be appropriate to many different situations. One would be hard-pressed to argue that principals should not be honest with teachers or model the behaviors they expect. All strategies require reflection. How often should modeling occur, under what circumstances, and to what degree?

To be applicable in restructured schools, other strategies require more critical reflection. When will praise, for example, be perceived as sincere and motivating, and when will it be perceived as condescending? At least one teacher in our study was angry at her principal's frequent use of praise. She wondered why the principal did not see her as a professional who was motivated by the work itself, with no need for external verbal reinforcement. Each school and each teacher presents a unique context for the person in the formal position of leader. Knowing when a particular set of behaviors is appropriate requires many on-the-spot conversations. No how-to book can alleviate the need for reflection in action—reflection that includes understanding the political, social, and interpersonal dynamics of the situation.

Similarly, no action, once taken, is educative without further reflection on that action and its consequences. Schön (1983) cautions that without both reflection in and on action, professionals resort to routinized performance that is necessarily less effective in new circumstances with new problems of practice. Dewey (1963), too, warns that experience can be "mis-educative" if not followed by deliberate attempts (through reflection) to link the new experience to earlier ones and to other forms of knowledge.

Unfortunately, because of the constant demands that need immediate attention by principals, reflection on action does not always follow reflection in action, at least not to the degree that principals tell us they would like to see. Once a decision is made and actions are taken, principals may not have the time later to evaluate that event. The conscious recording of alternatives that were considered, choices that were made, and consequences of actions taken may not take place. For this reason, it is difficult for effective principals to share what it is they do that makes them effective. Researchers who explain the effective principalship solely from the perspective of the principal, therefore, may not fully capture the art and science of school leadership. Thus, the use of multiple perspectives, such as the teachers' viewpoints presented in this book, may have considerable value.

Similarly, research methodologies based on perceptions (principals' or teachers') of behavior may overemphasize the strategies of effective leaders but largely ignore the thought processes such leaders use in selecting those strategies. We may be able to determine what some leaders do in some contexts that is effective for some teachers, but we may slight the important on-the-spot reflection that contributes to the decision to do whatever was done. Thus, the knowledge gained from study of the behaviors of effective principals is useful to inform practice, but only if placed in the hands of the leader also skilled in the processes of reflection—both in and on action.

Reflection "In" and "On" the Future

Many would argue that schools are slow to change. We have all heard the complaints that what we teach and the way we teach it are not very different than when we were students. Although progress may be slow, there has been a push in recent years to alter leadership in schools radically. Alternately termed *restructuring* and *site-based management,* the new emphasis is on decision making at the school level. Those most affected by decisions—administrators, teachers, and parents—are "empowered" to make critical choices about the structure and process of schooling.

The literature on school restructuring offers much hope for a demoralized teaching profession. Unfortunately, it offers little direction. Because few schools, if any, have been restructured in the fullest sense, there is little evidence of the movement's success. More important, there are few clues as to how professionals actually interact in restructured settings. The ideal picture has been painted, but the ideal has not been realized. District and community expectations constrain radical attempts at change. Further, teachers and administrators are themselves uncomfortable with such dramatic shifts in roles (Weiss, 1990). Hence, the "wave" of reform has consisted of sporadic trials with mixed results. There is mounting evidence that without careful planning for implementation, the restructuring movement will not be accepted by the people it is intended to empower.

The Challenge

Although the efforts of school reformers are generally sincere, and the commitment of school practitioners to new processes of governance is authentic, such change in schools presents all concerned parties with a number of profound challenges. What will constitute effective and dynamic leadership in the schools of the future? What kinds of leadership purposes and strategies will help facilitate the transformation from bureaucratic to shared governance structures? If administrators do not support change, or if their actions are even unintentionally inconsistent with the intended goals and processes, such change will most likely fail. Can the knowledge gleaned from leader behaviors in the schools studied today assist us in preparing leaders for the schools of tomorrow?

What are some basic assumptions regarding leadership in restructured schools? First, the formal authority of administrators would be diminished. Instead, their role would become increasingly facilitative; they would help provide the basic resources and avenues for teachers to accomplish the goals and objectives that are collectively determined. As such, strategies of influence—such as authority as we discuss it—probably would be less viable.

A second assumption about leadership in restructured schools is that a key role of administrators would become helping teachers to become leaders. Many administrators already use the strategy of involving teachers in decision making. Such involvement may be the first step toward greater teacher leadership. Delegation is one technique for involving teachers; unfortunately, though, many principals delegate to only a handful of teachers. As Roland Barth (1988) notes:

> Too often, the criterion for bestowing leadership on an individual is evidence that the person knows how to handle a problem. Yet innovative solutions come more often from teachers who don't know how to handle a problem but desire to learn. The moment of greatest learning for any of us comes when we confront a problem that we desperately want to resolve . . . This is the point at which leadership and staff development intersect. (p. 641)

Thus, it appears that involvement must be accompanied by continuous and meaningful professional development to be successful in achieving the goals of restructured schools—that is, of making teachers into leaders.

Although there are no easy recipes for effective leadership in restructured schools, perhaps we can begin to identify a framework to assist principals in developing a leadership approach that is most appropriate. To begin, administrators have to evaluate both the purposes and the strategies they use in their work with teachers. Do such purposes treat teachers as coleaders, or is there an underlying attempt to control teachers? Do the strategies facilitate teacher growth and professional development in ways that are consistent with teachers' needs and aspirations? In effect, are principals working with teachers to ensure that the ends of education (goals, purposes, etc.) and the means of education emerge from collaborative interaction with teachers?

Current theories and research on school leadership are inadequate in providing clear pictures of what administrators ought to do in restructured schools. Our own data are collected from teachers describing principals in today's schools; these schools did not approach the forms of collaborative governance envisioned for the future. Nevertheless, many of the strategies used by open and effective principals discussed throughout this book reveal assumptions about the purposes and processes of schooling consistent with the tenets of restructuring. Involvement and professional development, for example, although not pushed to their fullest, indicate an acceptance of the efficacy of teacher empowerment: Shared decisions are better than individual decisions, and informed group decisions are better than decisions based on incomplete knowledge.

We believe that many of the principals our teachers described led schools in various stages of transition. Eschewing any notion of autocracy, these principals cautiously, perhaps hesitantly, began to move toward more collaborative structures. How might we use our knowledge of the strategies of principals in transition to develop principals capable of leading truly restructured schools?

Armed with incomplete knowledge, thrust into unfamiliar settings, and confronted with unprecedented problems, the effective principal of the future will likely personify the reflective and moral practitioner. Experience enables the principal to see the new situation for its similarities to and differences from past events. Thus, experience is a guide in problem framing. Past understandings reinforced through practice and research enable the principal to formulate alternative solutions to complex problems. These alternatives are tested against prior knowledge; a preferred solution is selected, tried, and evaluated. This reflection in action is followed at a less demanding moment by reflection on action. What effect did the alternative(s) have? Is a similar situation likely to arise? Can similar consequences be expected? Were any unanticipated negative consequences associated with the actions taken? Has this action had the desired effect of shifting the locus of control over school processes from administrators to teachers? Only through this reflective process can a framework of effective leadership for restructured schools be developed.

In addition, the principal of successful schools will exemplify moral leadership (Sergiovanni, 1992). Although their strategies for improving schools may vary, they will use immutable principles regarding what's best for the children under their care as their "moral compass" (Covey, 1992, p. 94). Experience will be supplemented by research on what works in today's schools and, most important, what is best for all children, in formulating the knowledge base on which practitioners "reflect" in framing and resolving new problems. Using our data to represent one component of that knowledge base (principals' experiential learning, other research, and conventional wisdom are others), we can speculate on the kinds of questions the reflective practitioner might raise.

Let's examine the strategy of praise in the context of a restructured school. Suppose that faculty morale is particularly low. Attempts to implement a new parental involvement program have met with only minor success in spite of the vast amount of time and energy expended by teachers in designing the project. The faculty requests a meeting to discuss "next steps." What is the leader's role in this meeting? Our data suggest that today's principals capitalize on opportunities to praise teachers for their accomplishments. Is praise an appropriate strategy here to encourage teachers to continue their efforts?

A principal's reflective monologue regarding this situation might look like this:

> I should open the meeting with a comment on the teachers' hard work and dedication. But is that my role? They too are leaders; as such, they encourage one another. By their standards, their efforts have been unsuccessful. Don't patronize them.
>
> But my role is to facilitate. Praise can be motivating, thus facilitating further action. When teachers were frustrated by the failure of the tutorial program, they seemed to appreciate my attempts to minimize the negative effects.
>
> True. Praise can facilitate. But my primary role now is to develop leadership among teachers. Use strategies that achieve that goal. Perhaps praise is appropriate, but it should come from teachers. I should help teachers acknowledge their own successes.

With basic assumptions thus established, the principal can begin to take actions to assist teachers in recognizing their own strengths. Praise remains a viable strategy of influence, but the locus of control—the responsibility for praise—has shifted from administrator to teachers.

Principals who are able to act in the manner described above have been termed *transformational* (Bass, 1985; Burns, 1978; Leithwood & Jantzi, 1990; Leithwood et al., 1996). The transformational leader agitates the status quo by questioning existing assumptions and challenging others to reach new heights. Transformational princi-pals work to make teachers into leaders. The development of indi-vidual capacity is the primary leadership role. As such, transforma-tional leadership has a unique moral dimension.

Some of the principals that teachers described to us appear to be at the early stages of transforming schools and teachers. They encourage new forms of governance and expanded roles for teach-ers. The transformation envisioned for restructured schools, how-ever, is so different from traditional notions of schooling that few administrators and few teachers are fully prepared for their chang-ing roles. Given that little has changed in the structure and process of American education in more than three centuries, it is not surpris-ing that restructuring has not yet revolutionized public education. Considering early historical notions about the need to control teach-ers' lives (down to the number of petticoats they were permitted to wear!), the thought of teachers as professionals—indeed, as leaders in control of their own work—may appear ridiculous to some. Even so, education is easily influenced by promises of "quick fixes." (We have all criticized the pendulum syndrome.) Restructuring is to-day's promise, today's buzzword. Many district, school, and univer-sity programs are pushing the pendulum in that direction. Is there any hope of stopping the momentum of the pendulum's return?

We believe that two conditions are necessary for the successful restructuring of schools. The first is the kind of transformational leadership that many principals are beginning to learn. According to Burns (1978), transformational leaders help develop followers through individualized attention to their professional growth and challenges to the existing order. In schools, this would require viable alternatives to the traditional faculty in service: Individual needs are seldom met through activities designed for all. It would also require that needs and goals be mutually determined. Although some ad-ministrators will form committees for strategic planning and staff development, many will do so only in response to the moving pendulum. Their commitment is to improve perceptions, not to develop teachers. Our study suggests that some open and effective principals are committed to teacher development and collective decision making. The use of strategies such as involvement and support for teachers to attend professional functions indicates a move in the direction of transformational leadership.

The second condition necessary for successful restructuring is teachers' commitment to expanded roles and to increased account-ability. Of course, teacher commitment is directly related to leader intent. If the principal and other school and district administrators are perceived as "playing at" restructuring, teachers are unlikely to invest their time and energy in the game. If, however, teachers view the efforts as sincere and accept the challenge to become partners in school leadership, then the likelihood of real transformation im-proves. Many of the leaders described to us were perceived as honest and sincere in their commitment to school improvement. These personal characteristics that teachers associate with open and effective principals appear to be necessary qualities of leaders in restructured/transformed schools.

We believe that administrators have an obligation to provide opportunities for teacher growth, but we also hold teachers account-able for seizing those opportunities. Only by virtue of their ex-panded commitment and knowledge do teachers earn access to decision-making power. Teachers have traditionally been afforded access to neither decision-making nor individual learning opportu-nities. Paradoxically, once teachers are able and willing to assume leadership functions in schools, it would be unlikely that they could ever again be disempowered.

At this important juncture in the history of American education, school administrators face enormous challenges. Teacher leadership can be viewed as a key to improving the academic and social opportunities for students. Conversely, it might be viewed as a threat to the continuation of the principalship. Whether the school leaders of today view restructuring as a threat to their survival or as a promise for optimizing student growth will depend largely on their own values and character. Whether they "play at" restruc-turing or earnestly attempt transformation will depend on their political orientations and confidence in teachers. Our data suggest that many principals have already accepted the challenge to re-form schools. For others who are also sincere in their efforts to improve education for all participants, we offer the strategies of open and effective principals leading today's schools—those pio-neers who must balance simultaneous and conflicting external pres-sures both to control and to empower—as backdrops for reflective practice.

References

Barth, R. S. (1988). Principals, teachers, and school leadership. *Phi Delta Kappan, 69,* 639-642.

Barth, R. S. (1990). *Improving schools from within.* San Francisco: Jossey-Bass.

Bass, B. M. (1985). *Leadership and performance beyond expectations.* New York: Free Press.

Burns, J. M. (1978). *Leadership.* New York: Harper & Row.

Covey, S. R. (1992). *Principle-centered leadership.* New York: Simon & Schuster.

Dewey, J. (1963). *Experience and education.* New York: Macmillan.

Leithwood, K., & Jantzi, D. (1990, April). *Transformational leadership. How principals can help reform school cultures.* Paper presented at the annual meeting of the American Educational Research Association, Boston, MA.

Leithwood, K., Tomlinson, D., & Genge, M. (1996). Transformational school leadership. In K. Leithwood, J. Chapman, D. Corson, P. Hallinger, & A. Hart (Eds.), *International handbook of educational leadership and administration* (pp. 785-840). Boston: Kluwer.

Schön, D. A. (1983). *The reflective practitioner: How professionals think in action.* New York: Basic Books.

Schön, D. A. (1991). *The reflective turn: Case studies in and on educational practice.* New York: Teachers College Press.

Sergiovanni, T. J. (1992). *Moral leadership: Getting to the heart of school improvement.* San Francisco: Jossey-Bass.

Weiss, C. (1990, April). *How much shared leadership is there in public high schools?* Paper presented at the annual meeting of the American Educational Research Association, Boston, MA.

Wimpelberg, R. K., Teddlie, C., & Stringfield, S. (1989). Sensitivity to context: The past and present of effective schools research. *Educational Administration Quarterly, 25,* 82-107.

Resource A:
Research Methods
and Procedures

$\mathcal{T}$ he purpose of this book has been to focus on issues of practice. Some readers may be interested in a detailed account of how the data on which the book is based were collected and analyzed, however. A brief description is provided herewith.

Procedures for data collection and analysis were based in symbolic interaction theory. This methodological perspective emphasizes the interpretations and meanings that people construct in their particular social settings. The individual is viewed as a social product who is influenced by external factors (e.g., policies, superordinate leadership) but who also is capable of maintaining distance and is able to initiate individual action (Blumer, 1969; Mead, 1934). In contrast to some qualitative research perspectives, symbolic interactionism focuses on the structure of individual consciousness and perceptions (Blumer, 1969; Tesch, 1988).

Using this method, the study reported in this book employed open-ended questions and focused on the broad question, "What are teachers' definitions of the strategies school principals use to influence them?" Descriptive data relevant to understanding teachers' perspectives were collected.

The importance of perceptions to the topics identified previously is well-established in the leadership, micropolitics, and organizational power literature (Bacharach & Lawler, 1980; Ball, 1987; Burns, 1978; Hamilton & Biggart, 1985; Mangham, 1979; Pfeffer, 1981). The data were analyzed to generate categories, themes, conceptual understandings, and theoretical ideas.

Allport (1942) suggests that an open-ended questionnaire is a useful personal document for qualitative research that focuses on the subjective perceptions of people. Such an instrument is defined as "any self-revealing document that intentionally or unintentionally yields information regarding the structure, dynamics and functioning of the author's life" (p. xii). A *questionnaire* is defined as a personal document when the research participants exercise substantial control over the content of their responses. Questionnaires of this type have been employed successfully in other research (Blase, 1986, 1988; Blase & Pajak, 1986; Pajak & Blase, 1989).

An open-ended questionnaire, the Inventory of Strategies Used by Principals to Influence Teachers (ISUPIT), was designed to elicit free expression of personal meanings regarding the research topic. To develop the first version of the ISUPIT, the researcher consulted with a committee of three professors and five teachers. This instrument was piloted with 39 graduate students enrolled in education courses at a major state university. Suggestions made by the committee and students were considered in the construction of the final form of the instrument.

The ISUPIT consisted of three legal-size pages. On the first page, teachers provided general background information. They also rated their principals in terms of openness and effectiveness (on 7-point scales). On two additional pages, teachers were asked to provide detailed descriptions of two influence strategies used by their school principals. The specific questions were:

1. Describe and give a detailed example of a strategy or tactic (overt or covert; formal or informal; positive or negative) that your principal uses frequently to influence what you *do* or *think* in the school or in the classroom.

2. Describe and give an example of the *effects* (impact) that the strategy has on your *thinking* and *behavior* (if any).

3. Describe and illustrate what you believe to be your principal's *goals/purposes* in using the strategy identified above.

4. How *effective* is the strategy in getting you to think and do what the principal intended? (7-point scale) Please explain why.

5. What *feelings* (if any) do you have about your principal's use of this strategy?

Exploratory research of this nature is designed to produce data-based categories and conceptual understandings by increasing the variation among the research participants (Bogdan & Taylor, 1975; Glaser, 1978; Glaser & Strauss, 1967). Because of the open-ended design of the ISUPIT, the substantial time required for completion (about 40 minutes), and the sensitivity of the research topic to practitioners, a mailout survey was ruled out. Rather, 14 professors of education administered the ISUPIT between 1989 and 1990 to full-time public school teachers taking courses in five on- and off-campus centers of universities located in one southeastern, one northeastern, and one northwestern state. Involvement in this study was voluntary; teachers were not instructed to write their names on the research instrument.

Of the more than 1,200 respondents who completed the ISUPIT, 836 identified their principals as open, effective, and participatory on the 7-point scales provided (means were 5.7, 5.9, and 5.2, respectively). The remaining teachers described influence strategies used by principals who were perceived as relatively closed and ineffective. *This book presents only the open-effective portion of the data* (n = 836). The decision to discuss this portion of the database was founded on its theoretical, research, and practical significance.

The primary sample consisted of male (n = 172) and female (n = 664) teachers from rural (n = 292), suburban, (n = 443), and urban (n = 101) school locations. Elementary (n = 335), junior/middle (n = 284), and high school teachers (n = 217) participated. The average age of teachers was 37; the average years in teaching was 12. The sample included tenured (n = 714) and nontenured

(n = 122) teachers. Married (n = 669), single (n = 130), and divorced teachers (n = 37) participated. Degrees earned were BA/BS (n = 299), MEd/MA/MS/EdS (n = 523), and EdD/PhD (n = 14). The teachers described male (n = 497) and female principals (n = 339). The mean number of years with the current principal at the time of this study was 4.

The study sample is roughly consistent with the national distribution of teachers in terms of gender, age, degrees earned, and marital status. A slightly lower percentage of average years of experience, a lower percentage from urban locations and higher percentage from suburban locations, a lower percentage from elementary schools and higher percentage from junior/middle and high schools were represented in the sample, compared with the national distribution (National Education Association, 1983, 1990).

Data from the subsample of 836 teachers were coded according to principles for comparative analysis (Glaser, 1978; Glaser & Strauss, 1967). This procedure consisted of a comparison of each element coded previously in terms of emergent categories and subcategories. Line-by-line analysis of each questionnaire page (which included descriptions) produced 1,323 major strategies and a host of tactics (i.e., specific practices) related to each strategy. Subsequently, each strategy was analyzed within the context of the questionnaire items on the ISUPIT. That is, data related to effects on teacher thinking/behavior, principals' goals, effectiveness of strategies, and feelings were coded for categories and subcategories. Display matrices synthesizing each aspect of each strategy then were constructed (Miles & Huberman, 1984). These charts facilitated numerical analyses of strategies as well as further substantive analyses (e.g., effects on teachers). Comparisons across strategies were used to construct data-based conceptual and theoretical statements.

Each of the two questionnaire pages available to respondents was analyzed for only *one* strategy. In essence, the number of strategies coded is equal to the number of pages completed. In all, 836 teachers described 1,323 strategies used by principals with whom they worked and who they believed were open and effective.

The database was also inspected to determine if the use of certain influences strategies was linked to such characteristics as gender of the principals or teachers. Although discernible patterns were generated from this analysis, no conclusions were drawn.

One researcher analyzed the questionnaire data. This required approximately 800 hours. In addition, three professors and two doctoral students were consulted when questions arose. The doctoral students also inspected the descriptive matrices developed by the researcher. As noted, each matrix was designed to display different segments of raw data, thematic data, and data related to theoretical codes.

Consistent with the principles for inductive analysis, all the descriptive categories, themes, and conceptual ideas presented in this book were derived from data appearing on the ISUPIT.

References

Allport, G. (1942). *The use of personal documents in psychological science.* New York: Social Science Research Council.

Bacharach, S. B., & Lawler, E. J. (1980). *Power and politics in organizations: The social psychology of conflict, coalitions, and bargaining.* San Francisco: Jossey-Bass.

Ball, S. J. (1987). *The micro-politics of the school: Towards a theory of school organization.* London: Methuen.

Blase, J. (1986). A qualitative analysis of sources of teacher stress: Consequences for performance. *American Educational Research Journal, 23*(1), 13-40.

Blase, J. (1988). The politics of favoritism: A qualitative analysis of the teachers' perspective. *Educational Administrative Quarterly, 24*(2), 152-177.

Blase, J., & Pajak, E. (1986). The impact of teachers' worklife on personal life: A qualitative analysis. *Alberta Journal of Educational Research, 32*(4), 307-322.

Blumer, H. (1969). *Symbolic interactionism: Perspective and method.* Englewood Cliffs, NJ: Prentice Hall.

Bogdan, R., & Taylor, S. (1975). *Introduction to qualitative research methods: A phenomenological approach to the social sciences.* New York: John Wiley.

Burns, J. M. (1978). *Leadership.* New York: Harper & Row.

Glaser, B. (1978). *Theoretical sensitivity: Advances in the methodology of grounded theory.* Mill Valley, CA: Sociology Press.

Glaser, B. G., & Strauss, A. L. (1967). *The discovery of grounded theory: Strategies for qualitative research.* Chicago: Aldine.

Hamilton, G. G., & Biggart, N. W. (1985). Why people obey: Theoretical observations on power and obedience in complex organizations. *Sociological Perspectives, 28*(1), 3-28.

Mangham, I. (1979). *The politics of organizational change.* Westport, CT: Greenwood.

Mead, G. H. (1934). *Mind, self and society.* Chicago: University of Chicago Press.

Miles, M. B., & Huberman, A. M. (1984). *Qualitative data analysis: A sourcebook of new methods.* Beverly Hills, CA: Sage.

National Education Association. (1983). *The national teacher opinion poll* [Research memo]. Washington, DC: Author.

National Education Association. (1990). *Estimates of school statistics.* West Haven, CT: Author.

Pajak, E., & Blase, J. (1989). The impact of teacher's personal lives on professional role enactment. *American Educational Research Journal, 26*(2), 283-310.

Pfeffer, J. (1981). *Power in organizations.* Marshfield, MA: Pitman.

Tesch, R. (1988, April). *The contribution of a qualitative method: Phenomenological research.* Paper presented at the annual meeting of the American Educational Research Association, New Orleans, LA.

Index

Abilene Paradox, 49-50
Achilles, C. M., 5
Ackerman, R. H., 26, 64, 70
Administrative support, 119-120.
    See also Teacher development,
    enhancing
Adult learning, 69-70
Advice. *See* Intervention
Agreement:
    management of, 50-52, 55
    mismanagement of, 50
Allen, L., 4, 43, 84
Allport, G., 132
American Association of School
    Administrators, 107-108
American Educational Research
    Association, 1990 meeting of,
    47
Anderson, G., 107
Andrews, R. L., 70, 113
Argyris, C., 96
Armor, D., 27
Austin, G. R., 24
Authority:
    accepted uses of, 98-100
    appropriate times for exercis-
        ing, 103
    direct, 98
    effect on teachers, 99-100

limited consultative approach,
    99
selective use of, 101-103, 120
teacher compliance, 100
See also Formal authority
Authority paradox, 60
Autonomy, teacher, 60, 120
    as delimited, 62
    attitude and, 64
    freedom from close inspection,
        61-63
    freedom to teach as desired, 63-
        64
    implications for practice, 65-66
    in curriculum/instructional de-
        cisions, 60, 64
    in methods of instruction, 60
    in resource allocation, 60
    in student evaluation proce-
        dures, 60
    in time use, 60
    performance and, 64
    strategies for encouraging, 62
    types of, 60-61

Bacharach, S., 42
Bacharach, S. B., 60, 132
Ball, S. J., 132

Bamberger, P., 60
Bamburg, J. D., 113
Barth, R. S., 121, 125
Bass, B. M., 77, 106, 110, 127
Bauer, S., 60
Beady, C., 23
Beck, L. G., 12, 96, 107
Begley, R., 3
Biggart, N. W., 132
Blake, R., 110
Blanchard, K., 96, 97, 103, 110
Blase, J., 2, 4, 5, 12, 13, 16, 27, 29,
    42, 62, 70, 72, 85, 87, 89, 107,
    113, 132
Blase, J. R., 2, 5, 12, 13, 42, 62, 70,
    72, 87
Blumberg, A., 2, 4, 5, 85
Blumer, H., 131
Bogdan, R., 133
Bolman, L. G., 107
Bossert, S., 2
Brady, L., 2, 4
Bredeson, P. V., 4, 5, 27
Brookover, W., 2, 23
Brown, B. L., 4
Burns, J. M., 127, 128, 132

Charisma, 4, 106
Charismatic relationship, 106
Choral yelling, 29
Classroom management skills,
    monitoring/developing, 80
Clift, R., 87
Collaboration, 42
Collaborative leadership, 96
Collegiality, 49
Communication forums, principal-
    teacher, 36
  chance encounters, 36
  drop-in, 33
  formal conferences (individual),
    32
  formal conferences (small-
    group), 32
  general faculty meetings, 32, 36
  informal meetings, 33

  newsletters, 33, 36
  private memos, 33, 36
  student assemblies, 36
Competence, influence and, 107
Conger, J. A., 5
Congry-Oseguera, P., 27
Conley, D. T., 62
Conley, S., 42
Conley, S. C., 60
Cousins, B., 3
Covey, S. R., 126
Cox, M., 27
Crow, G. M., 4

da Costa, J. L., 4, 42
Deal, T., 12
Deal, T. E., 107
Decision making, participatory, 4, 5
  advantages of, 45-46
  faculty unity and, 43, 44
  fostering support and, 43, 44-45
  quality of decisions, 43
  suggestions for effective, 55-56
  teacher attitudes toward, 46-48
  teacher effort and, 48-49
  teacher morale and, 43, 44
  teacher performance and, 48
  See also Decision making, strate-
    gies for involving teachers in
Decision making, school-level, 124
Decision making, strategies for in-
    volving teachers in, 49-54, 120
  formal, 52-53
  impromptu, 54
  informal, 53-54
  See also Abilene Paradox
Dedick, R., 27
Delegation, 54, 119, 125
Dembo, M. H., 27
Desselle, S., 24
Dewey, J., 122
Direct instruction, 28
Discipline. See Student discipline
Donaldson, G. A., 26, 64, 70
Donaldson, G. A., Jr., 60
Dunlap, D., 62

Dunlap, D. M., 97
Dwyer, D., 2

Eckley, M., 19
Edmonds, R., 23, 72
Edmonds, R. R., 2
Effective programs, identifying strategies from, 34-35
Effective schools research, 1
Efficacy, teaching, 26-27
Empowerment, teacher, 19, 42
  power in, 87-91
  See also Research literature, dissemination of; Teacher development, enhancing
Enabling, 5
Evaluating, 2
Evers, C. W., 12, 107
Expectancy statements, 25
Expectations, language of principals', 31-32
  clarification, 31, 32, 33, 36
  consistency, 31, 32, 36
  repetition, 31, 32, 33, 36
  See also Expectations, principals'; Modeling behavior
Expectations, principals', 35-36, 83, 120
  curriculum and, 28
  generalize, 36
  guidelines for effective use of, 35-37
  program goals, 28
  student achievement and, 23-24
  teacher attitude and, 24, 29-31
  teacher behavior and, 24-25, 27-28, 29-31
  teacher-parent communication and, 28
  teaching methods and, 28
  See also Communication forums, principal-teacher; Leadership through expectation
Expertise, 4, 5, 25
Exploratory learning, 28

Faculty cohesiveness, teacher morale and, 44
Faculty participation, 43
  advisory, 54
  facilitating effective, 55-56
  formal strategies, 52-53
  impromptu, 54
  informal, 53-54
Falkowski, C., 23
Feedback, 41-42
  after classroom visits, 114
  personalize, 36
Fiedler, F., 110
Firestone, W. A., 4
Flat structures, 42
Flood, P., 23
Formal authority, 95-97
  detailed lesson planning and, 100-101, 102
  effective use of, 97-100
  grading practices and, 101, 102
  negative effect, 100-101
  sign-in sheets and, 100, 102
  See also Authority
Foster, W., 107
French, J. R. P., 103

Garvue, R., 24
Genge, M., 5, 90, 100, 112, 121, 127
Georgia schools, vii, ix, 43
Gibson, S., 27
Glaser, B., 133, 134
Glaser, B. G., 133, 134
Glenn, B., 23
Glickman, C., 4, 43, 84
Glickman, C. D., 42, 43, 52, 69, 96
Goal setting, 2
Goldman, P., 62
Gordon, S. P., 69
Greenfield, W., 2, 4, 5, 12
Greer, J. T., 4

Haertel, G. D., 64, 70, 72
Hallinger, P., 2, 3, 24, 46, 56
Hamilton, G. G., 132

Hannaway, L., 2
Hanson, M., 4, 5
Harvey, J. B., 49, 50
Hawley, W. D., 87
Heck, R. H., 2, 3, 24, 42, 72, 76
Hensley, F., 4, 43, 84
Hersey, P., 96, 97, 103, 110
Hickory Hills Elementary School
    (GA), vii, ix
High, R., 5
Hipp, K. A., 27
Hodgkinson, C., 107
Holland, P., 87
Honesty:
    influence and, 107
    of effective principals, 109-110,
        111, 115, 120
Hord, S. M., 70, 76
Hoy, W. K., 4, 27, 59, 60
Huberman, A. M., 134
Human relations skills, 4

Influence strategies. See Expecta-
    tions, principals'; Praise of
    teachers, principal's
Inspiration, influence and, 107
Instructional climate, 2, 3
Instructional leaders:
    collaborative strategies, 43
    principals as, 12
Instructional leadership, 12
Instructional materials/supplies,
    principal as provider of, 70-72
Instructional organization, 2
    leadership behaviors and, 2-3
Instructional time, protecting, 75-
    76
    limiting faculty meetings, 75, 80
    reducing paperwork, 75, 80
    teacher behavior and, 76
International Congress on School
    Effectiveness, Second, 46
Intervention:
    appropriate, 84-85
    direct, 84-85

importance of language used,
    86, 92
indirect, 86-87
informal conversation, 86
interpersonal diplomacy, 86
suggestion, 85-87, 120
suggestion versus intruding,
    92-93
training opportunities, 92
See also Teacher development,
    enhancing
Inventory of Strategies Used by
    Principals to Influence Teach-
    ers (ISUPIT), 132-133, 134, 135
Involvement strategy practices:
    delegation, 119
    formal team structures, 119
    open-door policy, 119
    solicitation of suggestions, 119
Isherwood, G. B., 4
Isolation, teacher, 69

Jantzi, D., 4, 5, 89, 90, 127
Johnson, M., 87
Johnson, N. A., 4
Johnston, G. S., 5
Joyce, B., 76

Kanungo, R. N., 5
King, N., 27
Kirby, P. C., 48, 70, 87
Kouzes, J. M., 27, 44, 106, 107, 113

Lakomski, G., 107
Larsen, T. J., 2, 24, 42, 72, 76
Lasserre, C., 27
Lawler, E. E., III, 106
Lawler, E. J., 132
Leader effectiveness, personality
    and, 106
Leaders, personality of, 108-111
    considerate, 110-111, 115, 120
    honest, 109-110, 111, 115, 120
    optimistic, 108-109, 111, 115, 116,
        120

Leadership:
  consideration-based, 107
  honesty-based, 107
  optimism-based, 107
Leadership through expectation, 26
Leadership through support/
    incentives, 78-80. *See also* Teacher development, enhancing
Lee, G., 2
Lee, V., 27
Leinberger, P., 1
Leithwood, K., 3, 4, 5, 89, 90, 100, 112, 121, 127
Lezotte, L., 2
Lieberman, A., 16
Lortie, D. C., 16
Louis, K. S., 12, 55, 70, 96

Maeroff, G. I., 42, 87
Mangham, I., 132
Marcoulides, G. A., 3, 24, 42, 72, 76
Marshalek, B., 24
Marshall, C., 107
Matthews, L. J., 4
Maugham, B., 23
Maurer, S., 2, 32
Mazzarella, J. A., 2, 32
McCleary, L. E., 4
McDonnell, L., 27
McLean, T., 23
Mead, G. H., 131
Meyer, J. W., 61, 62
Miles, M. B., 134
Miller, D. M., 110
Miller, L., 16
Miskel, C. G., 59, 60
Mitman, A., 24
Modeling behaviors/attitudes, 2, 34-35, 37, 105, 111-112, 115, 120
  expected behaviors, 112
Monitoring, 2
Morale building, 76-78, 83. *See also* Praise, teachers' reactions to; Praise of teachers, principal's
Moral leaders, 107
  principals as, 107-108, 115 126

Moral leadership, 126-127
  ethic of caring and, 116
Mortimore, P., 23
Mouton, J., 110
Murphy, J., 2, 12, 24, 70, 96, 107
Muth, R., 4
Myth of professionalism, 62
  changing to reality, 64-65

Natemeyer, W. E., 96, 97, 103
National Education Association, 134
Noddings, N., 96, 97, 107
Norm setting, 5

Observation, 17
Okeafor, K. R., 62
Ouston, J., 23

Pajak, E., 132
Parks, D. J., 76
Participatory management, 42
Pascal, A., 27
Patterson, J. A., 107
Pauly, E., 27
Peer coaching, 17, 28
Pendulum syndrome, 128
People-centering, 42
People orientation, 110
Personal example, 4-5
Persuasion, 4
Peters, T., 102
Peterson, K., 2, 12
Pfeffer, J., 132
Posner, B. Z., 27, 44, 106, 107, 113
Power, 44-45
  bases of, 96
  expandability of, 45
  informal, 4
Praise, teachers' reactions to, 14-15
  confidence, 14
  dedication, 14, 15
  instructional practices, 15
  loyalty, 14
  modeling with students, 15
  morale, 15

motivation, 14
pride, 14
satisfaction, 14
self-esteem, 14
sense of belonging, 14
support for principal, 15
Praise of students, teachers', 26
directed, 26
Praise of teachers, 11-13, 83, 120
as influence strategy, 13-19, 43
boasting, 20
brief, 21
faculty cohesiveness and, 13
frequency of, 19
goals associated with, 13
group praise, 17-18
in restructured schools, 127
indirect, 18
individual praise, 18, 19
informal, 18, 19
instructional performance and, 13
maximizing nonverbal, 20
nonverbal gestures, 18-19
opportunities for, 17-18
potency of, 16
principals' underuse of, 12
scheduling, 20
school climate and, 13, 15
sincerity of, 19-20
support for school goals and, 13
variety of, 19
work-related, 17, 21
written, 18, 20
Principals:
as counselors/parents, 12
as instructional leaders, 12
as mirrors, 111, 115
as models for teachers, 111
as moral leaders, 107-108, 115
as nurturers, 12
as supervisors, 12
female, 96, 97
school culture and, xi, 5
See also Leaders, personality of;
Principals, effective
Principals, effective, 123
characteristics of, 120

Professional development conferences, providing for teacher
attendance at, 71, 79
Pruyn, P., 24
Purkey, S. C., 23

Raven, B. H., 103
Referent power, 106. See also
Charisma
Reflection in action, 121-122, 123
Reflective practitioner, 121-122, 126
Reiss, F., 4
Reitzug, U. C., 2
Research literature, dissemination
of, 34, 89-91, 93
Resources, distribution of, 5
Respect:
for students, 26-27
Restructured schools:
assumptions regarding leader-
ship in, 124-125
strategy of praise in, 127
See also School restructuring
Richardson, D., 56
Rinehart, J. S., 19, 87
Riordan, G., 4, 42
Roberts, J., 4
Rogers, D. L., 107
Rosenblum, S., 55
Rosenholtz, S., 16
Rosenholtz, S. J., 60, 61, 65
Ross-Gordon, J. M., 69
Rossmiller, R. A., 55
Rowan, B., 2, 61, 62
Russell, J. S., 2, 32
Rutter, M., 23

Safir, L., 75
Safire, W., 75
Schlechty, P. C., 42
Schmuck, P. A., 97
Schon, D. A., 121, 122
School-based decision making:
teacher empowerment strate-
gies, 43
teacher involvement strategies, 43

School-based leadership, 4
School choice, 96
School climate, praise and, 13, 15
School culture:
  collaborative, 5
  effective, 5
  healthy, xi
  innovative, 5
  toxic, xi
School effectiveness:
  expressive aspect, 110
  instrumental aspect, 110
School improvement programs, improved teacher support of, 71
School leadership, strong factors, 2
School reform, 1, 124
School restructuring, 123
  necessary conditions for, 128-129
  rationale for, 42
Schools:
  high-achieving, 42
  low-achieving, 42
  See also Restructured schools
Schweitzer, J., 23
"Seeding," 85
Seligman, M. E. P., 108, 109, 116
Sergiovanni, T. J., 5, 96, 121, 126
Shakeshaft, C., 96
Shared decision making, 42, 48
  advantages of, 45-46
  as time-consuming, 45
  See also Decision making, participatory; Decision making, strategies for involving teachers in
Shared governance, 42
Sheppard, B., 5, 24, 113
Short, P. M., 4, 19, 87
Short, R. J., 19
Showers, B., 76
Simpson, C., 16
Site-based management, 124
Situational leadership theory, 97, 103
Smith, A., 23
Smith, J., 27
Smith, M. S., 23
Soder, R., 70, 113

Steele, J. R., 107
Stevens, K., 2
Stogdill, R., 110
Strauss, A. L., 133, 134
Stringfield, S., 23, 70, 121
Student achievement:
  high expectations and, 23-24
  leader behavior and, 3
  principal expectations and, 24
Student discipline:
  consistent, 73, 74
  fair, 74
  positive approaches to, 73
  principal supporting teachers in, 70, 72-74, 78, 79-80, 120
  schoolwide policy, 79-80

Taylor, S., 133
Teacher behavior, influencing, 27-28
Teacher development, enhancing, 5, 69-70, 83, 88-89
  formal training sessions, 88, 89
  informal assistance, 88
  material/financial support, 70-72, 78, 79, 120
  protecting instructional time, 70, 75-76, 78, 80, 120
  student discipline support, 70, 72-74, 78, 79-80, 120
  tangible incentives, 70, 76-78, 80
  See also Professional development conferences; Research literature, dissemination of
Teacher efficacy, 27
  principals' actions and, 27
Teacher leadership, 129
Teacher loyalty, participatory decision making and, 5
Teacher performance, faculty involvement and, 48
Teachers:
  attitudes toward involvement, 46-48
  fostering collaborative relationships among, 4
  principals' influence on, 4-5

See also Praise, teachers' reactions to; Teacher behavior, influencing; Teacher development, enhancing; Teacher efficacy; Teacher leadership; Teacher loyalty, participatory decision making and; Teacher performance, faculty involvement and
Teams, 52-53
  dedication to, 49
  problems addressed by, 53
  structures, 52
Teamwork, 42
Teddlie, C., 23, 62, 70, 121
Tesch, R., 131
Tomlinson, D., 5, 90, 100, 112, 121, 127
Transformational leaders, 127-128
Transformational leadership, 100, 112, 128
Treslan, D. L., 4
Trust building, 4
Tschannen-Moran, M., 27, 110
Tucker, B., 1

Uline, C. L., 110
University of Oregon, 2

van der Bogert, R., 26, 64, 70

Veal, M. L., 87
Venable, B. P., 5
Visibility, principal, 105, 112-115, 116, 120
  effects of, 113
  in classrooms, 113-114
  in hallways, 113, 114
  innovativeness and, 113
  motivational effect, 114
  professional involvement and, 113
  teacher commitment and, 113

Walberg, H. J., 64, 70, 72
Wang, M. C., 64, 70, 72
Weber, M., 106
Weil, M., 24
Weiss, C., 47, 56, 87, 124
White, T., 2, 32
Whole-school perspective, 47
Willower, D., 107
Wilson, B. L., 4
Wimpelberg, R., 70, 121
Wisenbaker, J., 23
Wolcott, H., 2
Women's Educational Equity Act Publishing Center, 97
Woolfolk, A. E., 27

Zellman, G., 27

CORWIN
PRESS

The Corwin Press logo—a raven striding across an open book—represents the happy union of courage and learning. We are a professional-level publisher of books and journals for K–12 educators, and we are committed to creating and providing resources that embody these qualities. Corwin's motto is "Success for All Learners."